CHOICES *FOR SUCCESS*

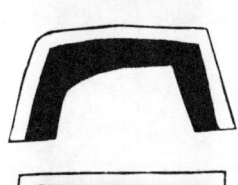

FOR SUCCESS

Your happiness in your own hands

Judith Orloff-Falk
Peg Doubleday
with *Alexa Cloud-Guest*

CollinsDove
A Division of HarperCollins*Publishers*

Published by Collins Dove
A Division of HarperCollins*Publishers* (Australia) Pty Ltd
22-24 Joseph Street
North Blackburn, Victoria 3130

First published 1991

Designed by William Hung
Cover design by William Hung
Illustrations by Sarah Wilkins
Typeset by Collins Dove Desktop
Printed in Australia by Griffin Press Pty Ltd.

The National Library of Australia
Cataloguing-in-Publication Data:

Orloff-Falk, Judy.
Choices for success : your happiness in your own hands.

ISBN 0 85924 932 8

1. Success. 2. Self-realization (Psychology). I. Doubleday, Peg.
II. Cloud-Guest, Alexa. III. Title.

CONTENTS

ACKNOWLEDGEMENTS

We want to thank our parents for choosing to keep us, for teaching us what they know, for loving us no matter what, and then letting us go.

We want to thank our families and friends, in particular our husbands and children, for challenging us, being stubborn, putting up with us, and giving us a reason to continue living in the midst of our deepest chaos.

We want to acknowledge all our past and present co-workers.

We want to acknowledge the inspiration of R. Buckminster Fuller, Teilhard De Chardin, and Stephen King as the metaphysical bases for the information contained in this book.

And most important, we especially thank all the people who have done our Choices programs through the years. We learned most of this from our association with you.

FOREWORD

I commend this book to all of you who seek your heart's desire but feel stymied at getting there. It is directed toward those of you who want to change those aspects of your life that you do not like and that do not work for you. The unique, central and recurrent theme is that of taking full responsibility for your life now so that you can choose and direct the changes that you want to make. Real change always involves a stretch, and this model invites you to choose how far you will go. These methods work for people who have committed themselves to the challenge and the excitement of change.

It has been my privilege and pleasure to have been associated with Judith Orloff-Falk and Peg Doubleday for the past five years. I have myself used their methods effectively for change and subsequently with dozens of people with whom I have worked as a Choices teacher and as a psychiatrist in both Hawaii and California.

I am delighted that the Choices information will now be available as a readable text. The message will be understood by all of you who are seeking your own experience of personal change.

The material is neither esoteric, abstract nor clinical. It is down to earth and so straightforward that the reader will find it both fascinating and personally engaging. Each of you will recognize aspects of yourselves in most if not all of the topics presented.

This book is intended to be used and referred to often, to be marked up and given to friends. I hope it will become both your guide and companion on the most fascinating journey of your life, your personally chosen and directed change.

Jay M. Jackman MD

1
— CHAPTER —
INTRODUCTION

We all have a *purpose,* our soul's reason for being born. Living that purpose creates immense joy and freedom. Some of us remember our purpose and some of us do not. When we were children, we had a connection with our purpose. It was as natural to us as breathing. It served as a backdrop for the games we played, the books we read, the people we were drawn to, the dreams we had and the feelings and thoughts that seemed to come out of nowhere. Most of us have lost that connection, in fact some of us may not even remember we had it. But without it, it does not matter how much money and power we accumulate, most of us are conscious of something missing, an ache, a loneliness, and we will create crisis after crisis in an effort to find the missing piece.

This book will help you discover and *reconnect with your purpose.* It will teach you the theories and give you the practical experiences that will be a foundation for living a life of joy and freedom. In order to accomplish this successfully, we need to understand that the knowledge of the nature of our purpose can only come from inside our hearts and souls. We start the process of accessing that information very simply.

We commit ourselves to doing it — no matter what.

Committing means that we say what we mean and we mean what we say. This is no "will of the wisp" decision that we change as soon as the going gets tough.

And the going does seem tough some of the time. Committing can create strong feelings of panic, nausea and anger and it can also create deep peace. No matter what the feeling, however, our commitment always creates a window of opportunity. Our strong intention to do what we said we would do stands beside our com-

1

mitment and carries us through the feelings of panic or confusion. This focus of will called intention is like a laser and will be very important when we want to deny what we know in the process. Finding other committed people to aid us in our times of denial is also necessary. These people will risk themselves by telling us what they see and feel about how we are doing. They will help us to maintain our integrity, to make sure we have one face. So making sure we have strong intention and true support keeps the commitment alive every day. By doing this with all our heart, we begin to experience freedom. This book defines freedom as the inner commitment and outward behavior to keep our word, no matter what we feel or what we think, and telling ourselves the truth, even if that truth does not fit our pictures. *We are free to be who we choose to be* despite the pressure from inside and out to compromise ourselves.

In the natural order of things we grow up and our purpose translates itself into a vision and a mission. A vision is the picture of our purpose brought to life. If we live our purpose, what will be the result? For example, our purpose may be *to help people*. Our vision therefore could be *a safe world*. Our mission is what we will do to manifest our vision, for instance *by being a firefighter*. As a firefighter we will do our best to ensure people's safety when there are fires. In that way we fulfill our purpose of helping people and work towards our vision of a safe world. There are an infinite number of ways to fulfill the purpose of helping people and there are a lot of possible visions of what helping people would create. And not too strangely there seems to be a group of purposes that many of us have in common.

Sometimes our purpose, vision and mission are clear and steady, like that of the child who knows his or her purpose is to be a healer, and has a vision of a world without pain, follows this course without hesitation into medical school and then moves to the inner city to work with the homeless.

Sometimes we lose sight of our purpose, and then a personal crisis, such as a parent becoming ill or dying, may occur and enlighten our path to our purpose, and vision and mission. We also may go to medical school to be a healer but instead of being a physician in the inner city, we may work as a research scientist and develop medicines for curing disease.

And some of us may stay unaware of our purpose throughout our entire lives, stumbling on it time and time again and not even noticing it under our feet.

Because of the constant bombardment from external stimuli in our environment, it is often difficult to recognize that one of our primary needs is to chart our own course: to be connected with and to actively trust our inner self, to believe and to live our heart's desire and soul's purpose. By taking the initiative to do this we choose freedom, rather than living out a desire for outside approval. Rather than seeking acknowledgement of what we do and who we are, we learn to make clear choices, which raise our self-esteem and build our confidence in our own ability.

In order to forge a direct pathway to clear choice it is necessary to eliminate our negative childhood beliefs (such as "I'm not worth that much" or "I can't make up my mind" or "I'm not smart"). Beliefs are what we unquestioningly think is true about us and the world according to what was demonstrated by our parents. And we are often mistaken in what they taught us about what they believed. What parent truly believes their child is not worth much? If you are a parent, can you imagine believing that about your child?

So that we can live our commitment to our purpose we need to further understand both the theory and concepts of how choice works, and the practical skills that will make us the experts about making choices for ourselves. Once we have this knowledge and know how to use it, we will know for sure if the path we are on is one that leads us to fulfill our purpose and lead a joyful life. We can have a clear vision of where we are going and how to get past our internal obstacles to get there.

All of us have stored in our cells, consciously or unconsciously, every experience we have ever had. The unconscious effects of these experiences are still steering us. For example we are always looking for the "right" person to be with. This search comes from our desire to recreate our parents. Our patterns of relationship and intimacy stem from our original family. We loved them no matter what they were like or what they did, and we are loyal to how we thought they wanted us to be. That loyalty comes from the child within us, our inner child. It is usually not even the truth of what they wanted. But as children we interpreted what they said and did to mean certain things and *very few of us ever checked it out.*

We still interpret everything. And if we are not in touch with how we use our beliefs to interpret what happens, then we do not see ourselves as the source of our experience. Without that way of seeing ourselves, we do not accurately know what is going on around us. In fact, we are handicapped. We are stuck with the same responses to life that we have always had, thinking that those responses are caused by someone else or some external event. If we are willing, however, to be personally responsible for our thoughts, feelings and actions and the results we create in our lives, we will be liberated from our history. We can choose how we will be in the face of anything. Exercising that responsibility creates unconditional love for ourselves. We can forgive ourselves and everyone else in our lives for all the mistakes we all made and understand how we came to make them. We can learn compassion.

Unconditional love and personal responsibility are the cornerstones of the new reality coming about in our evolution at this time. They are tools that will enable humanity to pull itself back from the disasters that seem to threaten us on all sides and instead create a world of love and joy, and a world where we are free.

How to use this book

The information in this book has been in the testing stage for twenty-five years. In our work with thousands of people just like you, and in our own personal lives, we have discovered over and over that unless someone has a personal *experience* of a theory or application of information it only sits in the head. The greatest benefit you can get from this book is to *use it* — to do all the exercises, to feel everything that gets stirred up in you as you read.

We learn by a combination of theory and experience, and that is the way the book is written. Each section has text and exercises. Some of the exercises are to be completed in a few minutes as you read the book. Others will take some time to accomplish. As you do them, the information will make more and more sense and will generate new information in you.

Reading this book, doing the exercises and using the information will throw you into *paradox*. You will be having apparently contradictory feelings, thoughts and experiences at the same time. The old patterning of your childhood and this new information will appear at times to be at odds. To achieve freedom and permanent change the trick is *to stay with the paradox*. Paradox is where true change can happen, by holding the old and new at the same time, by feeling all your feelings, thinking all your thoughts and staying committed to your purpose, vision and mission all at the same time. Sounds like quite a feat. But if you think that you can grow by dealing with just one side or the other you are mistaken. If, on the one hand, you try to abandon your past and take on the information in this book without deeply searching for the validity of the past, you will be deceiving yourself. You will be living in an illusion. Growth does not happen like that. You need to experience your past in the light of new information. That process works like alchemy — it creates wisdom. If, on the other hand, you ignore this opportunity for change and stay doing what you have always done, hoping for the best, your soul will not let you be satisfied. It wants you to live a joyful life no matter what you have done in the past, no matter what you think. This book offers one path to that. If you discard this opportunity another will just present itself to you later.

The richest, most fertile way to use this book is to let it drive you a little crazy for a while until you create a new pattern for yourself from inside, from your *heart, mind and soul*.

This book, if used as we suggest, will help you change your patterns and core beliefs to make your life successful and free. All these beliefs and patterns were learned in early childhood, some even in the womb. So as you read each section and do the exercises, you will experience strong feelings and may have vivid memories of your early years. In fact, you can expect this. As we change our reality, we feel resistance. And that is natural and normal. Remember, we were part of a family system and that system kept us alive. In fact, it brought us to the place of being willing to read this book. When you honestly change part of that system, you will experience great agitation. That is a good sign in terms of change. Enjoy!

To prepare yourself for reading this book, we begin with a guided meditation. Please read it twice — once for understanding, and once for experience.

Guided meditation

Close your eyes and get comfortable. Float backwards in time. Feel yourself drift back to your past. You may feel like you are spinning. Go way, way back, before you had a body, before conception, back to when you were just a spirit.

Now from that space of being a spirit, create inside of you a triangle, a pyramid with a floor, made of white light — of unconditional love. Walk into your pyramid. Call in the spirits of your mother and father. Ask your parents why they want you; why they have chosen you? Ask your spirit why you want them as parents and trust the answer you get. Ask yourself what is the lesson that you are here to learn from them. Ask your spirit what your purpose is for being here. For this life.

Then let your parents go. Let the white light and the pyramids disappear. But keep your awareness of your purpose. Let yourself know what it was like when you were conceived. Allow yourself to go into the womb. Remember what it felt like to be in there. Remember you are more than just a body, you are also spirit... watching... feeling... seeing. Let yourself feel how it is to grow inside the womb. Feel everything; experience whatever is going on.

It is time for you to be born. You are being born to accomplish a purpose. Let yourself feel what it is like being born even if there is anesthesia. Know you have chosen to be born. Let your senses experience your birth. Let yourself know the birth you have chosen is the first step in accomplishing your purpose. Is your birth "natural"; is it a Caesarian; are forceps being used? Why have you chosen this birth? What do you see first when you are born? What do you taste, hear, feel? Was it easy? Was it hard? Did it feel good — or not?

Let yourself know if you have made any decisions about yourself or your life now you are born.

Now come back to the present time, very slowly. Keep your eyes closed. Feel the ground here. Move your toes and start to feel your body here. Move your arms, legs, feet. Open your eyes. Look around. Stand up. Shake the body out. Take a little walk if you need to, but make sure that you are here, so you can go on. Remember your purpose.

PART

CHILDHOOD

1

We come into life with an undiluted love for our parents, for life and for ourselves. We are in a state of unimpaired ability — integrity. We are exactly what we are. We do not pretend. We do not judge ourselves or anyone else. We are totally responsive and receptive to life.

Birth is our first experience as a separate physical being. Our passage through the birth canal gives us an imprint of our physical boundaries. (Babies born by Caesarian section do not have this experience and have great difficulty with setting boundaries. It has been possible in many cases to heal that problem. One way we have discovered to compensate for a Caesarian birth is to surround yourself or the child with pillows, mold them to your body and sleep that way for at least a month.)

Whatever our birth experience it seems to set the stage for the way we see life. If our birth was a long difficult one we might tend to see life as difficult. If our mother was anesthetized we might tend to be unaware of things. If our birth was easy, we might tend to expect that our life will be easy. Birth, however, is not the only factor determining how we deal with life as an adult but the physical experience of birth lays down the framework, a matrix for learning.

Infants are brilliant. For instance, we are born able to experience life as it truly is. We can mimic a smile within eighteen hours of birth. While still in the womb we know the sounds of our parents' voices, we respond to stressful situations consciously, and can even learn to recognize different music.

Children learn instantly. As children we adapted to a ritual as soon as it happened. The first time our parents did something with us, it became a ritual. We were conscious throughout most of our life in the womb and by the time we were one year old, we understood the world around us and how it worked. We knew how our parents or the people taking care of us dealt with life. And we survived, and in most cases, flourished.

Children do not mistake any experience. They experience the truth of every situation and experience everything — what is said and meant, what is not said, and all the uncomfortable feelings that parents are having and are not necessarily experiencing. For example they know when parents are fighting even though they may be silent.

Frank and Melissa were in their early twenties. They had married because Melissa was pregnant and were not happy staying married. Their baby, six-month-old Jeremy, was clearly aware of the tension. He would spend hours reaching out his arms to one parent, snuggling into their neck and being adorable and then immediately reaching out to the other parent and doing the same thing. He repeated the pattern over and over as if he could physically knit their relationship back together. He was clearly aware of the potential break-up of his parents' relationship and was doing everything a six-month-old could do to keep them together.

The patterns that control and direct our adult lives are formed before we are two years old. We learn by that time which feelings are permissible in our families and which are not. We learn to hide the feelings that our parents find intolerable or we may get sick, become apathetic or feel abused. We learn how to take care of their emotions — we act in ways that allow them to take the focus off themselves and focus their emotions on us. We provide them with reasons to live and to love. We learn the "culture" of our particular worlds and make sure we pass it on to our siblings, friends and everyone we meet in the way we act. We believe what our parents believe and then we forget they are beliefs. We think and act as though our beliefs are the truth about the world.

We are very busy during those first two years. Yet even with all this work and busyness that we go through, there is still lots of room for being happy and joyful.

2
━ CHAPTER ━
BLISS

Bliss—the highest happiness

When we were small, we had time to play, we could love freely and we seemed to be more intrinsically ourselves. We had space to daydream, to imagine unknown futures and to create joy with few props.

Why are we less joyful now than when we were young? Let us first look at how we became less blissful.

Just bliss

True bliss is very different than being "blissed out" or finding a way to escape from who we are and the world around us. Bliss has been described in many different ways. In this book it is referred to as a "sea of bliss"; the philosopher Franklin Merrell Wolff called it a "transparency"; and Christians call it "a state of grace" — but whatever term is used, all suggest that bliss is part of the experience of unconditional love for ourselves and others.

Bliss

True bliss is the ability to accept all of life's experiences equally, whether we feel happy or sad, fearful or joyful, angry or loving.

This is how we all were most of the time when we were less than six months old — it is the infant state of adult joy. So how can we recognize bliss? Apart from deep joy, we feel big and fulfilled and expansive — we have the sense of a lack of physical boundaries and an intense feeling of well-being. It is almost as if our organs have disappeared and there is just clear space inside our bodies. Most importantly we are not separate from any living thing.

Most of us still have some blissful moments — and they feel wonderful. Many of these times are connected to being in love or having a child. And we usually think that these moments are caused by some event or person outside ourselves, or even that they are accidental or random. We look at these wonderful moments the same way as we look at the horrible ones — as happening *to* us. We do not usually see ourselves as the *source* of our experience, our feelings, our thoughts or even our behavior.

From bliss to less bliss

Even though each of our lives is unique, we all lost the abundance of bliss in the same way. We learned fear and forgot who we were.

At first, in the womb and immediately after birth, all we experienced was bliss and physical sensations.

As infants, we swam in the sea of bliss.

Each sensation was equal and just passed through us. Our facial expressions changed every few seconds. Nothing stuck. We had one face. The inside showed immediately on the outside.

EXERCISE: Spend time watching and being with babies under six months old. Notice how you feel around them and how quickly they move from one sensation to the next.

13

Sea of bliss

Sensations

As humans our bodies first receive experiences as sensations. Think of all the sensations our bodies have — softness and tightening, emptiness and fullness, burning and bubbling are some. There can also be physical pressure, heat, coolness and many others.

EXERCISE: Take ten minutes and just notice the different sensations in your body.

When we were very young, we experienced only pure sensations. You see, sensations belong only to the moment; no part of them is derived from the past.

Interpretation — from sensation to feeling

Very early in our lives we learned to call these sensations feelings and to give them names such as fear, happiness, sadness and many others. The particular interpretation that we give to any sensation is generally the way it is interpreted in our families. The sensation of heat or a quickening pulse, for instance, can be called anything from anger or hate, to excitement or thrill. Once we named the sensation as a feeling, it stuck and created a small island in the sea of bliss.

14

Sensations to feelings

**Now in the sea of bliss we have our sensations and the
way we learned to interpret them — our feelings.**

Sea of bliss with sensations and feelings

15

There are universal sensations as well as cultural responses from a particular experience. Most people, especially children, will experience the sensation of warmth and be heart-touched from viewing a Lassie film or any story about an animal saving a child's life. How we as adults interpret that sensation and the depth of the heart-touch will depend on our particular family history and our cultures.

Pattern development

When we start interpreting any sensation one particular way, it becomes the first link in our pattern of response to life as it was in our families.

So the next step in pattern development is guided by the responses we got when we displayed our feelings. When we were babies and felt hungry, we cried for food. When we were angry or afraid, we screamed; happy — laughed or smiled. We acted exactly the way we were feeling! We had one face and it was transparent.

Our parents or the adults around us responded when we displayed those feelings. Their response either reinforced or inhibited us, depending on how they felt when we behaved the way we did. They sent us messages based on how they dealt with those particular feelings. We learned from them which feelings were good to have and which were not. We developed unique ways to mask particular feelings from ourselves and others that were not okay.

As we masked the true feelings and sensations in increasingly complex ways, the sea of bliss flowed further away.

Whatever was repeated and reinforced, became a habit, a pattern — a framework to hold future interpretations and beliefs. For example, if in our families fear was typically met with disapproval, our parents may have tried to stop it directly or indirectly by distracting us. Or they may have become frightened themselves and shown it through anger. If we ran out into the street, for instance,

16

our parents may have shouted at us angrily instead of showing how afraid they were. This sets up the framework for fear being expressed as anger. So whenever we feel afraid, we will express it as anger without our even knowing it. After any pattern response is set, whatever we encounter in our lives we will be compartmentalised into that patterned response.

The sea of bliss became filled with sensations and feelings. Every time what we were feeling was denied by our parents, we changed our experience rather than risked the hurt of being separate from them. Every masked sensation and feeling became an island that separated us from the sea of bliss.

Some feelings became so thoroughly protected from hurt that eventually we forgot the original experience. The sea of bliss got crowded with protection.

The sea of bliss gets crowded

And now when these feelings arise within us, our protection, defense, or reaction, is all we can access. Furthermore, each year of our lives we have experiences that reinforce our childhood patterns so that they appear so tightly woven as to be almost impenetrable and unrelated.

Judgement

What happened next was a very important part of how we got along in our families — our survival *depended on it*. As children we were totally dependent on our parents. We *had to* conform to how they wanted us to be. We were afraid they would leave us or stop taking care of us if we did not. And we could not stand being separate from them. We remembered their responses to a certain feeling, and gradually we began to think about and experience the feeling in the same way they did.

We learned very quickly, before we could speak, or understand the words that were spoken to us, whether a feeling was acceptable or not. This was taught to us as judgement. It became normal to us. And we experienced this judgement as factual. This layer of thought that surrounds the physical sensation and our feeling is the final step in the framework that sets our response pattern for our lives.

Peg: My middle son told me a few years ago that as a child he was always afraid to be angry with me. He was afraid that I would hurt him physically. So whenever he was angry, he would change it to hurt. This is exactly what I felt and did with my father.

EXERCISE: Think about what feelings were not okay in your family and what you used as a substitute for those feelings.

The judgement about certain feelings just went straight into our hearts. As children we believed and needed our parents' perspectives, no matter what! As a judgement about anger, for instance was repeated many times, our own patterns started to solidify. And today, we most likely find it difficult to accept anger and to simply feel it.

Judgements distract us from knowing what the truth is.

Not every family has the same judgement about every feeling. Your mother and father may enjoy their anger and their fights, and in that case you probably learned to associate anger with safety and connection. Some families may not judge their feelings and just accept them all equally — although this is very unusual! As it is unusual for people to have sensations without interpreting them as feelings, it is also unusual for us to have feelings without our judging them. But it is not as difficult as it may seem.

Peg: My youngest son, who is seven, is learning to be angry with me. He's having such a good time telling me off. I see all the times with my other children when I would have stopped them and judged their behavior as rude and inappropriate. My judgement was only my interpretation of my feeling of fear.

He is the first of my children to be able to share his anger with me. With tender care and good role modelling, he'll later be able to be angry with people in his life in a way that won't get him in trouble.

Judgement and illusion as protection

Let us say we are feeling happy in a family where there is also a lot of fear. In that family, our feelings of unreserved happiness and excitement may be met with certain uneasiness — a message not necessarily expressed verbally.

Even though our family is delighted with our being happy, the underlying message, which we all detect as children, may be "watch out, it won't last" or "one never knows what's around the corner". So our happiness, mixed with fear, becomes coated with the thoughts that happiness is not totally welcomed, not 100 per cent okay. There is a judgement about happiness — happiness is dangerous.

We absorb the happiness, the fear and the judgement all at the same time. The judgement about happiness serves to warn us, to protect us against all the disappointment experienced by our families for generations. Remember that when we were children we absorbed everything from our parents into our hearts. This is how we absorbed the emotional histories of our families.

As we grow up we expect that our families, friends and our lives are supposed to be a certain way. Then we behave in a way that assumes that our expectations are correct.

By the time we are adults, these patterns are solidified into our belief systems. Our beliefs set the ground rules for our behavior, and in most cases we are not aware of them and do not question them. We live on automatic pilot according to those rules. So for example, a person whose birth was long and difficult may have a framework for life being a struggle. Then say that this person's parents, because of the rough birth, are afraid of losing him or her yet not wanting to feel that fear. The parents would react to any imagined danger to the child by being over-protective and unconsciously train the child to be timid, fearful and not trusting of the physical world or of strong emotions. As those patterns solidified into beliefs, the child would simply believe that they were fragile, that life was hard and that they had to be careful.

As adults our experiences will continue to reinforce our childhood patterns and beliefs until we have an experience that does not match them. We create a shelter for ourselves from the feelings of conflict between what we believe or expect should happen, and what has in fact happened. This way of being is the birth of illusion. For example when someone we love no longer acts a certain way towards us, we can pretend we no longer care about them.

Illusion

If our experiences and beliefs do not match, we surround ourselves with a little pocket of protection, an illusion of what is true.

It is not unusual to protect ourselves when something happens which we do not like, rather than be willing to be vulnerable and experience just what is true.

Reaction

Reaction is the umbrella term for all forms of protection in our lives. It is what we do when we behave in the way we have learned in order to protect ourselves. Reaction is unconscious and takes many forms. It is a master of disguise. For example, if someone says something sarcastic to us, we may laugh instead of feeling hurt. The laughter in that case is our protection to cover up our hurt. Reactions are the alternative to feeling and sharing our feelings. They were our way to survive in our families' systems.

Reactions are our way to survive now when any part of us feels threatened and we are not aware of the underlying feeling that the reaction is protecting.

There are as many different types of reaction as there are families. If we felt intense happiness in the family where it was not okay to feel 100 per cent happy, we may have reacted by acting reserved or cautious and block the full emotion. When this happens, the happiness simply dissipates. Many people who respond to love this way are alone and often feel disappointed. They are unaware of any happiness that flows through them or comes their way.

The patterns are set by us

When we were children, we absorbed the original patterns of sensation-feeling-reaction from the thoughts around us. Although as adults we may like to attribute our personalities to our families and certain events in childhood, the exact set of patterns we each have is uniquely ours. Our reactions come out of our individual experience of our parents' judgement of what is or is not okay. We form our patterns from the ones we think are true.

Our deepest beliefs about ourselves often arise from misinterpretations of our parents' words and attitudes.

We develop our habits and personalities based on our original patterns. We have patterns for eating, sleeping and loving. In fact just about every aspect of our lives is part of a tapestry.

When our patterns are set we believe that life is a certain way and we prove it to ourselves over and over again. That is how we keep creating the same situations with different people. That is also how we stay protected *thinking* **we are safe.**

EXERCISE: In the table below are examples of some patterns — from sensations to feelings (interpreted sensation), judgements and reactions. See whether any of the patterns feel familiar to you. Use these patterns as a guide to start discovering some of the patterns in your life.

Sensation	Feeling	Judgement	Reaction
burning	anger	not okay	blame
pressure	fear	not okay	numb/hysteria
warmth	love	not okay	caution/sexual pleasure
emptiness	needy	not okay	isolation/bingeing
full	happy	not okay	fat/not eating
tingling	excitement	okay	no reaction
tingling	turned on	not okay	fighting

Remember that our beliefs, values, judgements and behaviors come from whatever served us best in our families and cultures. Different families value different feelings and behaviors. For example a family who were pioneer settlers many generations ago would value keeping "a stiff upper lip". To them, passion was dangerous. Being aware of feelings was not a high priority at that time because people had to have all their energy focused on survival, and feelings might be judged as weakness. Families from the Mediterranean area, however, value feeling in a different way. People from this area tend to argue a lot, have strong opinions and are passionate in their everyday life. In this case, not feeling may be judged as being weak.

By the simple act of choosing to observe our patterns and judgements in our everyday life adventures, we begin our personal odyssey and start creating the life we desire.

Beliefs

Our beliefs are part of a whole system or network of thoughts that originate from our basic patterning. For instance, look at the patterning table above. The sensation of burning was interpreted as the feeling "anger" and judged as being "not okay". So whenever we felt angry, we probably automatically began blaming someone or something. Out of that pattern comes many beliefs such as "anger is dangerous", "things don't bother me much" or "people are not to be trusted...". Further we may believe that we need to be careful around angry people and the most insidious effect is that we fail to recognize our own anger so we may say something like, "I am not angry" when we are.

Beliefs become our sacred cows of "reality". They are an unquestioning acceptance of something as true without positive knowledge or proof, as handed down by our family or environment.

Beliefs

23

We might want to eliminate our beliefs but we are human and we function through our ego, our belief systems. Because beliefs are an intrinsic part of how we operate, they have a creative force and they function to mold our reality.

Most of us usually do not spend much time assessing whether or not certain beliefs are okay. Yet the judgements and beliefs that we absorbed from our families and cultures are probably the biggest single factor that has determined our lives. While much of what we have learned has served us well, some has not.

One direct route to freedom is to learn how to discover what is true now, create a purpose, vision and mission, learn how to make choices, decide what you want to change and then do it, no matter what you think and feel.

Beliefs are just beliefs — they are not TRUTHS. Remember that we can change our beliefs by repatterning our behavior so it works towards creating joy and personal freedom rather than fear and separation. The following exercise is designed for you to start identifying some of your beliefs.

EXERCISE: Ask yourself: "What do I think is true about the world, my family, sex, love, children, parents, men and women, money, success, and power?" Then pick some more. Write down under each heading what your beliefs are. Then ask yourself: "Do these beliefs serve me in my purpose, vision and mission?"

Why do we not automatically take on the beliefs that are the most fun?! The reason we do not without strong conscious intention is that the creation of new beliefs causes conflict with the past. There is always the feeling of loss when we let go of our history, when we stop being loyal sons and daughters, when we start to parent our inner child ourselves.

EXERCISE: To get an idea of the matrix of your particular family, fill out the following table. Ask your family to help you complete the details. Ask them about their

24

most important and favorite memories. Ask what their childhoods were like.

What was important in my family? **What was not okay?**

_____ _____

_____ _____

_____

What are the happiest memories? **What are the hardest?**

_____ _____

_____ _____

_____

What was my father's childhood like? **My mother's childhood?**

_____ _____

_____ _____

_____

EXERCISE: If one or both of your parents are no longer alive, you can do this exercise this way. Send a form letter to as many people as possible (at least 20) — your parent's friends and relatives. Ask them to send you all kinds of information about what your parent(s) was like. This is so that you have not only your point of view but you can also gain the broadest perspective.

When you have completed the exercises, look at what you learned about your families along the way. What patterns do you notice? For example, my family valued each other and mistrusted everyone else. Be compassionate with yourself regarding any upset you feel along the way.

All the bliss we ever felt and more can be regained as soon as we create new ways to respond to the myriad of stimuli both inside and outside ourselves. It is truly a matter of choice. This book is about how to regain that bliss.

3
━━ CHAPTER ━━
FEELINGS

Introduction

For the purposes of clarity, the word "feeling" will be used throughout the book to mean "interpreted sensation". Feelings are the language of our hearts and the wisdom of our souls. Even though we are unable to see them with our eyes or touch them with our bodies, our feelings are how we connect with ourselves and the rest of the world.

When we completely feel a feeling, from any experience, we learn the information from that experience and it cannot be forgotten. We understand what is really true about ourselves and the particular situation. We learn how to live without deceiving ourselves, without illusion. This form of learning teaches us through our bodies from the inside out. We grow. Because that feeling permeates every cell in our bodies and feeds our hunger for connection, it lets us know that we are not separate.

When we do not feel our feelings completely we are separate. We do not see what is true in that moment, we live in our heads and interpret the situation based on one that happened before in a way that usually handicaps us, and we miss out on one of our deepest sources of pleasure and learning. We do not feel our lives deeply because we are not in the present moment — we are somewhere else, usually with our original families. And we do not even know it!

What are feelings?

In their physical form, feelings are energy and they move like light — that is, they are both moving and vibrating at the same time. Feelings can exist as waves and matter.

Feelings are waves and matter

Remember a time when you felt sad and did not know why? And you cried and cried until you felt cleansed? Why when you were finished crying did you feel so good, so loving? You probably did not have a clear incident to attach it to until you finished crying. You probably did not judge yourself or anyone else. You probably felt the feeling all the way and the wave just passed through your body. That is your natural way of being.

When we are open to all our experiences, our feelings flow through us like waves in the ocean — as they pass through they vibrate inside us like a tuning fork vibrates with a piano. When we allow them to be whatever they are, we seem to become transparent and they move through us and go on their way.

When we are unwilling to experience feelings as they really are in the moment, our ability to vibrate or resonate with them is impaired. Instead of moving through us like waves, they get stuck inside us as matter. They do not disappear. They slow down and become a perversion of the original sensation and are instrumental in creating disease and violence. For instance, anger not expressed could be one of the causes of cancer.

Why don't we feel all feelings?

We learned our family's pattern of feelings. We learned which experiences were acceptable and which were not.

Judith: In my family, if we didn't argue about almost everything, we were not okay. On the other hand, if my feelings got hurt in school, or when playing with a friend, my family got angry at me for being sad or feeling hurt. Pure joy was always questioned and judged as being naive. It took me a very long time to be able to feel sadness without getting judgemental and angry; and to feel joy and pleasure without starting a fight.

Whenever our parents felt uncomfortable with what we were feeling and doing, they protected us and themselves from experiencing what was true. They wanted to control our pain or our anger and sometimes even our excitement and joy. They did not know that the reason they did this was because their own pain, anger or fear of loss was being activated by the waves of energy that were our feelings. This need for control happens with everyone when some feeling is activated that is not okay with them.

Mark's father died when he was five years old. It happened in a moment — he had a heart attack and was gone. The family was shocked and afraid. In order to protect Mark and his siblings, Mark's mother pretended that everything was okay. She would go into her room at night and cry when she was alone. Mark learned to be nonchalant when shocked and afraid and now has a very difficult time dealing with what is true.

All feelings are equal and different

All feelings are equal. How is that possible? How is it possible that sadness is equal to anger or joy? How can we stop judging our feelings as right or wrong? How can we stop interpreting what others are meaning?

All feelings come from a "bliss-like" state called unconditional love. Unconditional love is like white light. White light is made up of and contains all the other colors of light. Each feeling has its own frequency, its own color, and each is experienced differently. None is right or wrong, good or bad. They are just energy that moves through our bodies. And they are all part of that birthright of unconditional love.

EXERCISE: Close your eyes and imagine a white light. Let yourself know that the white light is unconditional love. Then imagine a red light — let that be anger. Visualize a color for each of your feelings. When all those feelings are held by and included in you they blend into

the experience of unconditional love — the natural state of babies.

There is unconditional love in all families, no matter what. Remember when we mold our interpretations of our experience in order to be part of our families, we stop having our full range of feelings. Like white light passing through a prism, unconditional love becomes split into its components. Love becomes colored and conditional, even though its source is the full experience of pure unconditional love.

EXERCISE: Think about which feelings were not okay in your childhood. Which feelings do you now associate with love and close personal relationships? How was love demonstrated in your family? How do you demonstrate love in your relationships now?

Feelings not experienced, persist and control us

There are many childhood events that we want to leave behind so we cloud them up or we create pleasant illusions to cover up the

Feelings not experienced persist and control you

pain. When we do this we then forget in our conscious minds what happened. This can lead to disastrous results.

When any experience is changed and the feelings are diluted and dulled, the particles of matter do not go away. The particles build up and begin to control our behavior, albeit unconsciously.

Judith: My dad had a heart attack. As fear was not allowed in my family, they kept telling me that there was nothing to be afraid of. So I stopped feeling fear. My parents never felt their fear. However, fear is still inside me so that sometimes I am afraid to be in my house alone and start looking for robbers in my bedroom. I also imagine disastrous results from the common cold.

Because of the patterns of interpretation and protection we developed in childhood many of us have no idea what and when we are feeling. Instead, we "act out" our feelings. Acting out is when we feel something like sadness or anger or happiness and either do not know it or will not allow ourselves to experience it all the way. Instead the feelings explode or leak out in other ways. For instance, a child who is jealous of a new sibling is usually not allowed to feel that jealousy — instead they may stab the baby with crayons, twist the baby's foot through the bars of the crib or burn their own dolls.

A disadvantage of not feeling everything is that we misinterpret what is going on. This is deadly in our relationships and our businesses. Someone we are dealing with may feel angry and if we are not able to experience anger we may think they are sad or not notice — and act on that faulty information. The results can range from hurt feelings to a lost contract or a business failure. If we think our relationship is doing fine because we are not aware of our own loneliness, we could exist in a relationship for years unaware of our partner's loneliness — even when they try to get our attention by having an affair. Then we are very surprised when they leave. We do not understand why they left. We feel used or hurt. We say things such as: "I didn't do anything wrong." Misinterpreting feelings seriously damages relationships.

Wisdom

Many people want to skip the experiencing stage of their feelings — in fact some think it will kill them.

A man we will call Bruce watched his mother die slowly from cancer when he was a young boy. She took morphine until she was a vegetable. He took care of her and tried to stay in good spirits so she would not know how frightened he was. Eventually he forgot how frightened he was. He married a woman who was wonderful and loving. He provided the strength in their relationship. As they got to know each other, he did not want anything to go wrong so he stayed in good spirits whenever problems occurred. He was the same way as he had been with his mother — he denied that there were problems. His wife became afraid and anxious and started taking sleeping pills and drinking alcohol. He continued to deny there was a problem. His unexperienced fear of loss, anger and sadness about his mother guaranteed that he would have to relive the scene with someone else like his mother so that he could have another chance to feel those feelings. He stayed in the relationship until their fights became unbearable, they divorced, and he recently discovered he had cancer himself.

Usually we want to avoid "negative" feelings and go directly to the resolution of a problem. Staying with the experience of our feelings can be very uncomfortable. To relieve our discomfort, we try to control the experience by changing it — that is done by thinking it instead of feeling it. Eventually we call our thoughts "feelings" and we rarely have physical sensations except in extreme situations.

Feelings never leave the body until fully experienced.

Any original experience contains the seeds of learning. When it is planted, wisdom grows.

Judith: When I divorced my first husband, I had no idea that I only divorced him because I felt so deeply hurt. Instead I felt numb. I thought he was controlling, insensitive and didn't understand me. When we decided to divorce, I remember making a decision to act like I didn't care. I didn't want to let him know how hurt I was. I would not be vulnerable. If I had been willing to feel how hurt I was and to let him know, we could have stayed together. Our marriage was not a mistake.

Experience is the seed of wisdom

When we experience all feelings as equal, we can make our lives full and joyful, and see our families and friends as they really are. This is a key to freedom: just people, doing all they can to live life the best way they can, using the information they learned from childhood just as we are doing now.

Feeling everything in a relationship

When we begin a relationship there is usually a period of excitement, being on our best behavior, with all the romance of starting to get to know somebody. We experience ourselves and the other person as spontaneous and exciting or warm and tender. Then we develop an investment in holding on to the "good" feeling. Say, for instance, that we do not want to feel angry with this new person we are in love with. But if anger is there and the feeling is not experienced, that anger will persist and control us without our being aware of it. When we block out the feeling of anger we could instead experience a lack of sexual desire, or feel a little distant or look for the other's approval. The anger becomes disguised. It will not go away until we acknowledge it and feel it. We stop being ourselves and being able to see our partner clearly.

The relationship continues until we are at the stage where we are considering commitment. During this time some feelings will start to surface, which we think are unacceptable, especially if we really want to start a family and also want intimacy and connection. We will probably feel resistance, fear, indifference and anger, and will wonder if we really want to be with this person.

If we deny what is true in the relationship at the time those feelings and thoughts surface, something happens. We become immune to experiencing most of what is really happening because we have so much invested in controlling the relationship, in making it fit a certain picture. In addition, we will not feel okay saying what we do feel and experience. We may think: "If I say this, then he won't like me," and "If I act this way then she'll be upset."

How we decide to be at this time determines how the relationship will be.

If we hide and our partner does not consciously know it, then they are relating to someone who is hiding, a persona, our image. If they are aware that we are hiding, they will probably start to mistrust us. They will often begin to wonder whether we are lying or not. This pattern will pervade the relationship in all areas.

We continue to repeat all our patterns until we allow ourselves to have all of our feelings, especially the ones we do not like.

We do not want to experience anger because we are afraid it will threaten our feeling happy. Soon the feeling of anger fills us up and we experience less and less of our other feelings. The essence of our relationship becomes diffused anger. Trying to be happy when anger is inside, is a strain. We look "cheerful" and create separation between our inside and outside. We are then incongruent.

Our partners begin to mistrust their experience of being with us. So do we, although that experience is also dulled.

Even more destructive than that, however, is that we will not be able to experience our own sadness, our hurt, our anger. We will not be able to have the range of emotions that are part of the spectrum of unconditional love. Our passion goes out of the window and sex is terrible.

Our unexperienced anger starts to filter everything that we experience. Eventually we will be able to let in less and less that we can feel happy about. We think that the other person has changed and is not the one we really want to be with. We want to leave and find someone who is clearer, more responsible, more powerful.

The relationship becomes more and more of an illusion. That happens when the belief system creates the reality rather than the experience of what is true.

On some level we are aware of when we are living in an illusion, when the feelings inside do not match how we behave — when we are not congruent. The person who is covering their anger may unconsciously say "I feel fine" because they want to be liked. What "fine" means is "numb". We are not lying, we do feel fine — we are not lying to anyone except ourselves. It is impossible to really hide. Everyone knows when we are not being real.

George and Marion had been married for 20 years. They had a pattern in their relationship wherein he would have regular one-night stands after which he would come home and confess. Marion would be hurt and outraged and there would be a tremendous scene. George would be guilty and repentant. Then Marion would start asking questions about the other woman. She would be challenged to be a better lover. Their relationship would get wildly passionate for a while and then get dull again till George would have another affair.

The illusion was that Marion was being hurt and that George was a cad. The truth was that George had to have regular affairs to keep Marion interested. He was exhausted.

EXERCISE: For one week, keep a diary/journal of feelings you experience: your judgements of yourself for having those feelings; and your earliest memory of having them. Do not forget to be compassionate towards yourself.

4
⟨CHAPTER⟩
REACTION

Introduction

This chapter describes how and why we create negative patterns in our lives. These patterns of behavior are called reactions.

A reaction is the state of illusion that includes fear, projection, blame, justification, obsessive thinking, compulsive behavior and either/or choices (such as what is black or white, right or wrong). It encompasses all the ways we learned to act in childhood when our feelings were not okay with us or our families. That covers a large percentage of our lives.

So what is so important about reaction? We have an old response to something — so what? We think we are feeling one thing and we are really feeling something else — what difference does it make? We blame somebody or something for what we are feeling — is this so unusual?

Yes, most of us blame someone or something for what we are feeling. Many of us are not aware of what we are feeling and most of us respond to what happens now the way we did ten, twenty or thirty years ago. There's nothing "wrong" or "bad" with any of it.

It is just that we are at a disadvantage when we act this way. Our ability to assess present situations and relationships is impaired. We may be making decisions which we think are based on rational thinking when, in reality, they are based on emotions from past events that are unconsciously motivating our behaviors. And we will keep recreating our pasts. When we live our lives in reaction, we can be sure that our futures will be the same as our present and our past.

What is reaction?

Reaction is a loss of personal power. It is an unconscious or past response to a present situation. One way of thinking about a reaction is to imagine ourselves as a hedgehog. When threatened, a hedgehog raises its quills and rattles them ferociously. When danger passes, it lowers its quills. But because we develop unconscious patterns of behavior we often do not recognize when the outside situation changes. We keep rattling our quills at the outside, even if what is presented from that outside is love. We keep doing the things we did for our survival and protection even though they are not appropriate in the present.

"...defensive patterns are nothing more than misapplied and misplaced conditioned responses. The original stimulus is not there, so we fabricate it through this distortion of reality. Pathological defenses are again based upon humans doing what is familiar, not what is best."
(from The Causes and Prevention of Cancer, *by Dr Frederick B. Levenson, Stein and Day, 1985, page 79)*

Children, for instance, were brought from Viet Nam during the war to live in the United States. Every time these children heard a helicopter they would crawl into the safest hole they could find until the helicopter had gone — even though they were no longer in Viet Nam. When we feel threatened we think that the war is still on — that we still have to do certain things to save our lives.

reaction
feelings

Reactions are a cover-up

Why do reactions have so much power? We developed them initially to cover up those feelings whose expression was unacceptable. It was important for our survival that we get along in our families. The way we act to cover the feeling becomes the reaction. When we live in our reactions now, we are creating our lives and our relationships from our pasts, rather than from now. We are like a hedgehog that did not know that the danger ceased to exist a long time ago.

EXERCISE: Think about your childhood
1   **What feelings were unacceptable in your family?**
2   **How did you feel you had to behave with your mother?**

3   **How did you feel you had to behave with your father?**
4   **Do you feel you have to behave in those ways with anyone in a present relationship?**
5   **Does anyone in a present relationship have to behave that way with you?**

If you answered "yes" to (4) or (5), you are in reaction.

When we are in a reaction and act on it, the reaction is what we present to the outside.

We may, for instance meet someone who is very open and affectionate in expressing their love and we may want to have a relationship with this person. Yet we sometimes feel very uncomfortable and want to escape the company of someone so demonstrative with their love — when this happens, we are having a reaction! Why? We may have learned that it was okay to be only half-way affectionate, not all the way. So the result in our adult lives, if we are not aware of our reaction, is that even though we may feel deeply loving, the people closest to us receive only half of that love, and that half comes through the filter of our unconscious fear. Then we cannot understand why they are not satisfied because we honestly did our best to please them and to show our love.

What happens when you do not show all the love you feel

What triggers a reaction?

Say that we are having a great time now — we are even feeling blissful! Then our lover or partner confesses, for instance, that they are $25 000 in debt and have kept it secret, or that they are seriously attracted to another person. If that outside event activates feelings in us that are not acceptable, we will do whatever we used to do to mask those feelings. Instead of laughing or crying or whatever was our true experience we will leave our blissful state and start a fight.

Judith: My father gambled on the ball games and there were times he would be heavy in debt to his bookies. My mother didn't know about it and didn't want to know. Yet there was a fear of loss in our family and distrust of men being financially responsible. To this day I feel incredible panic if my husband doesn't do everything I tell him to do in terms of money.

An outside event simply acts as a trigger for a feeling inside that is not experienced and is covered over.

Acting out

One of the greatest myths about feelings is that if you feel it, you have to be or do it. Well, you do not. Often what we think of as feelings are just cover-ups. They are a step away from our feelings.

40

For example if we are angry and are unaware of it or think it is not okay to be angry, we might act it out instead. We may be nasty with people, have affairs, make a lot of mistakes at work, be frequently late or sick, or "accidentally" hurt ourselves. And still we will not know that we are angry. We may instead feel powerless and misunderstood, like a victim of circumstance.

EXERCISE: When have you felt powerless, misunderstood or like a victim? In those situations was there anything you were angry about?

If, on the other hand, you do experience your feelings, then you do not have to act on them. You are free to choose your behavior. Using the same example, you may feel angry and still do your job, treat people the way you choose to and be the way you want to be in your relationships. You may choose to tell someone what is going on but there will not be any blame in it and it is up to you. In other words, you can just feel that feeling and still go on living your life without acting on the feeling. Eventually, if you do not act out, you will really understand what the feeling means and the old history will be healed. If we continue to judge certain feelings as unacceptable however, we will probably attempt to avoid them through reaction. When we keep acting out, healing cannot occur.

Judith: When I was a little girl my father would be enraged when I was late. I was so frightened that I decided never to be late. Now I feel anxious and worried whenever anyone else is late and I'm kept waiting. However, for a long time I was not aware that I was worried and went into reaction in that situation. I acted nonchalant instead when the other person arrived. I wanted them to feel guilty. Those meetings often ended in a fight or at least, unresolved. Now I bring a book and love that inner child.

Projection

When we are "in reaction" in an illusion, we often cannot tell whether what we are feeling, seeing or experiencing is coming from outside or inside us.

A reaction is ultimately inside, about us, although we think it is on the outside.

Have you ever looked at another person and claimed that you know what they were thinking or feeling? Have you then asked that person and found out otherwise? Have you accused somebody and discovered that you had misinterpreted the situation, had misheard them or had attributed an incorrect motive for their behavior? And you were so sure you were right! This is called projection.

When we do not like our feelings, we have the ability to fool ourselves and think that they are coming from someone else. Then we blame and judge that "someone else" for the feelings we will not accept as our own. We end up giving up a lot of power and personal responsibility when we blame others for the reason we feel the way we do. And we experience ourselves as victims.

We are projecting a part of ourselves on to them when we are obsessed with someone else's behavior or motivation.

Imagine a movie camera, a projector, a film and a screen. The movie camera is inside our heads, recording what is happening. The film is all our unexperienced feelings, beliefs, fears — everything that we do not want to claim as belonging to us. We are always recording all events through our film, our filters. When we are in reaction, we project our filtered version of those events on to another person, event or institution — anything in the outside world.

The other person or thing is the screen we project on to. When we are projecting, we cannot see ourselves or the other. There is just someone or something out there to whom we attribute feelings, thoughts and motives. We cannot tell the difference between ourselves and the other because at that moment we do not want to know that it is we who are thinking those thoughts and deciding what their motives are — *we are so determined that it is about them!*

EXERCISE: Imagine seeing a slender, red-haired woman of thirty with a clear complexion and even features. Write down the thoughts that might pop into your head.

For example, you might think:

1 She probably dyes her hair.
2 I don't like her. She's prettier than I am.
3 I wonder what she's like in bed.
4 I'll bet she has quite a temper!
5 She's not that great. She looks stuck-up.

Projection

We all have parts of ourselves that we do not want to experience, which are often our most negative or most positive qualities. Most people take their dark side and project it outward, then are afraid of or repulsed by the person they put the dark side on. And some people take their very loving side and put it outside themselves; they are then jealous of or in love with that person.

These most positive and negative qualities are what we are in reaction to, what we fail to experience, and give away through projection.

Whether or not the other person has this attribute is of no particular importance. We can always justify or explain our reaction, and get evidence to prove that we are right about the other person. And we may be, but so what? Our reaction is about us. The other person just mirrors the projection.

43

EXERCISE: Make a list of each of the times in the last month you have said or thought "I think you..." Pay particular attention to those directed towards close family and friends. Complete the sentence for every occasion, and then substitute "I think I..." in the first part of the sentence. Do you recognize the matching part in yourself? Example: "I think you pretend to feel loving when you are not" changes to "I sometimes act loving when I am not feeling it."

An example of when we can give away or project our most positive qualities is when we "fall in love". When we have "fallen in love" we have such strong feelings. We think they are for and about the other person. We are swept off our feet by how much they understand us, their fabulous looks, charm, personality, etc. We think that the magic belongs to them. But consider this:

We are really talking about how we feel about ourselves in their company.

So if we think that someone is the most interesting, exciting, romantic and gorgeous person we have ever met, we actually feel that we are interesting, exciting, romantic and gorgeous in their company.

The magic comes from how we feel about *ourselves* and how open we are in the company of the other person. That is right; it is about how we feel about us!

That is why we can shift so rapidly from being in love to being in hate or being appalled that we are with this person — *our feelings have nothing to do with them!* This knowledge can carry us through the negative times of relationships.

The reaction is gone when we can see the other person clearly and as equal. This does not mean that the love dies — just that it becomes possible to have a relationship based on who both partners truly are in the moment, without any illusion. But what we often do when the illusion dies, when we feel the "magic has gone", is to think that the *other person* has changed and then dump them.

EXERCISE: Have you ever been "in love"? Remember your experiences and write down everything you thought about the other person. Look at the list again and imagine that you are describing yourself or how you feel about you. Now write down in a separate column how you feel when each item on the list is about you.

The more we see how our reactions and projections are about us, and are willing to learn from the information, the more powerful we become. Like all forms of reaction, projection puts us at a serious disadvantage in any negotiation, in any relationship, in any conflict.

Blame

Blame is a very powerful type of projection. When we are blaming, we are projecting a part of ourselves on to the other person and then judging them for it.

When we blame another person we become unable to learn from the situation because we cannot see how we contributed to its happening — we render ourselves powerless. In a sense we do not have all our wits about us to learn from, so then it becomes impossible to change.

Blame guarantees that a particular situation will continue in our lives.

One of the most intense situations in which blame will flourish is when couples separate. Usually when two people separate from a position of one blaming their partner, the person who is doing the blaming has to repeat the situation. They will usually find another partner to make it more obvious — to go through the same situation but even moreso than previously, so they can see how they created it from their own patterns. Everything in our lives recurs until it is fully understood, experienced and healed.

45

Judith: My last relationship ended unhappily for us both with plenty of blame going backwards and forwards. My experience was that I did all the work in the relationship, emotionally and physically. I blamed him for not wanting to share his life with me, not paying the bills on time, not cooking or taking an interest in how the household ran, etc. Several years later after I had married someone else, I was again doing a lot of the household work since he was renovating our house. All my own resistance and judgements about housework came along. I started nagging and blaming him. I thought that housework was menial and that I would be "trapped" in the house forever. I never knew before how much I wanted the other person to do everything! I realized then how much blame I had placed on my previous partner, and how little I saw my own role in our conflicts.

As I started to take back my projections and experience them as being about me, I saw how much work my partner did! I had placed so much attention on his being "wrong" that it was impossible for me to appreciate him.

EXERCISE: How do you most like to blame other people? Write a list of "I am... because...", for example: "I am late to the meeting because of the heavy traffic." Now there was heavy traffic and if it had not been that way, you would have been on time. But then ask yourself which feelings you did not want to experience, and whether there were any feelings you were unwilling to experience at that time, which you covered up by blaming someone or something?

Self-blame

The other side of blame, instead of blaming someone or something else, is to blame yourself: "I was a fool" or "I made her leave" or "I forced him to get fat". Self-blame and all forms of self-punishment guarantee that we will not be able to experience a situation fully and to learn from it.

Whenever we punish ourselves or someone else, all learning stops.

Reaction in action

How can you tell if you are "in reaction"? A reaction does not have to look a certain way. In fact, it will not. Since it is a learned behavior based on our *individual interpretations* of how we were supposed to be in our families, a reaction manifests itself differently for everyone. But here are some unmistakable clues. You may be "in reaction":

- whenever you think that what you feel is about someone else;
- when your mind will not shut up;
- when you are hiding or numb, feeling foggy or confused;
- whenever there is a judgement (good or bad);
- whenever you feel compelled to act or not act;
- whenever you have accumulated good evidence and can prove beyond a shadow of a doubt that you are right.

EXERCISE: Think of someone with whom you had, in the last few years, a fight that was never resolved.
What happens when you think of calling them to talk about it?
Please mark the responses you have:

- **I wouldn't give them the satisfaction.**
- **They'd never listen to me.**
- **I'd rather die.**
- **It's up to them to call me.**
- **What's the point of bringing it up after all this time?**
- **It doesn't bother me any more.**
- **I've already tried everything. Nothing works!**
- **It scares me but I think it's a good idea.**

If you marked any but the last response or did not mark any of them, there is a good chance that you are having a reaction. That is because these responses fit the criteria for a reaction, given at the beginning of the chapter.

You know that there is some feeling underneath that you are keeping as a secret from yourself. (Your friends, family and people around you, however, will experience your unfelt feelings).

Reactions are goldmines about ourselves.

How to get out of reaction

Make your reaction personal to you. Whatever events and stimuli happen outside of yourself are a catalyst for your feelings. Find out in you what your reaction is about. Mine the gold and invest it in the present.

How can you do that? How do you get out of reaction and *harvest the gold*? Here is a seven-step process:

1 Notice your thoughts and feelings. Are you blaming or justifying?
2 Choose to acknowledge that you are having a reaction.
3 Experience your feelings truthfully. What feelings are the reaction protecting?
4 Remind yourself that you are learning.
5 Be compassionate with yourself.
6 Experience the safety of vulnerability.
7 Choose unconditional love for yourself (no judgements).

Power lies in making all your reactions about you!

Reaction creates all the negative parts of society that people are ashamed and afraid of. Reaction creates violence of every type. Most crime against other people (and ourselves) is caused when people who are unused and unwilling to feel soft and vulnerable inside, become compelled to act tough on the outside to protect themselves. When people are not feeling what is true they are capable of creating any crime — people are not conscious then of what they are doing.

PART

FOUNDATIONS

2

So far we have discussed what happened to us that removed us from the natural experience of bliss, how our interpretations of things and our beliefs about life, combined with our love and loyalty to our families, limited our joy in life. We talked about what feelings are and how we cover up our true experiences through reaction.

The rest of this book is about how to regain that natural state of bliss. The next part goes into the *foundations* for living a life of joy: *personal responsibility*, where we are the source of our experience and *unconditional love*, where there is no judgement. These are the basis for the context of life that allows us the ability to re-pattern ourselves. Without seeing ourselves as the source we do not have enough personal power to make the change in our programing. And without letting go of judgement we will not have the compassion we need to truly see ourselves and our behaviors in order to know what to change.

5
━ C H A P T E R ━
RESPONSIBILITY

Introduction

"Alright! Who's responsible for this?"
"It's time to grow up and be responsible!"
"You can't do that! Think of your responsibilities!"

EXERCISE: What does the word "responsibility" mean to you? Spend ten minutes listing all the things in your life you associate with being responsible.

Responsibility means different things to different people. For a lot of us the word has negative connotations from our childhood. It is associated with blame and burden. For others it means power over people or being grown up.

True responsibility is the opposite of burden or control. It is the ultimate in personal power and the master key to freedom.

Success

We are all already creative and successful. We have created our lives to be exactly as they are in every way — as a combination of all our patterns, beliefs, judgements and intentions — both conscious and unconscious. Regardless of whether the results have brought us pain or joy, we have each created our lives from the moment of our conception. Furthermore, in each fleeting instant called the present, we continue to create. We continue to choose. We always choose our experience, present, future or past from an infinite number of possibilities, whether we "know" it or not.

Most of the time, these choices are like an automatic pilot. We choose according to our patterning and we do not even know it.

But consciously choosing to be personally responsible changes that. We start to know how we do it and we create unlimited options for choice. Responsibility is the essential ingredient of a successful adult life. Let's really look at what it means.

What is responsibility?

We were brought up with a lot of different meanings for the word "responsibility".

Webster's dictionary has at least six meanings, some of which are included here:

3. a particular burden of responsibility upon one who is responsible...
5. reliability or dependability, esp. in meeting debts or payments...
6. on one's own responsibility = on one's initiative or authority...
(Webster's Encyclopedic Unabridged Dictionary of the English Language, Portland House, New York, 1989.)

When we think of responsible people, we think about people who are reliable, pay bills on time, meet their commitments, tell the truth, and generally take care of themselves. People with these qualities are often called upon to represent others, say, in public office, and their lives are held up as models for others to follow.
In our culture, the word "responsible" sometimes carries a negative feeling, signifying a loss of freedom and increased rather than shared burdens. Responsibility may mean doing the "right" thing according to what you think is expected of you or simply from an unconscious loyalty to your own past — you have always done it this way, or thought that there were certain fixed ways of doing things that have been handed down from generation to generation. No wonder we think we are limited in the amount of choice and freedom we have.

Remember all the times we thought we "should" do something and in fact did it and later we felt angry and resentful? We did not experience the decision as a choice for us. In a life where the meaning of responsibility is a burden, full of "should", "must", and "have to" we generally end up feeling "trapped" in our life-style — by our jobs, family or friends. From this perspective, being separate is a reasonable and preferred choice.

"Responsibility" can also imply blame. So instead of saying "Who can I blame"? we ask "Who's responsible"? or "Whose fault is it"? And then the guilty party "owns up" as if they had done something wrong. Whoever is "responsible" gets blamed! So if we are responsible, then what else will we be blamed for? It makes sense from that picture to not be responsible in our lives at all. From this perspective, mistakes are not learning experiences, they are something to hide.

"Responsibility" also means that we live as reliable people who take care of ourselves. This is very important to our sense of self-respect. Furthermore, living responsibly creates a certain security derived from the act of responding in fixed or acceptable patterns. It is often not clear, however, whether we are living by these patterns from a need for approval, or whether we are living this way because we choose it. Looking to the outside world to approve or disapprove of us creates a sense of obligation and loss of freedom. From this perspective we are not capable of being joyful.

In this book responsibility means something else entirely. It means being free to *consciously* choose how we want to respond to any situation instead of being stuck with how we did things in the past. From this perspective, we are light and free and can fulfill our purpose.

"Responsibility" means both being able to respond in the moment as well as acknowledging yourself as the source of your experience. Within this context you can create a life of unlimited joy and freedom — a life time of adventure!

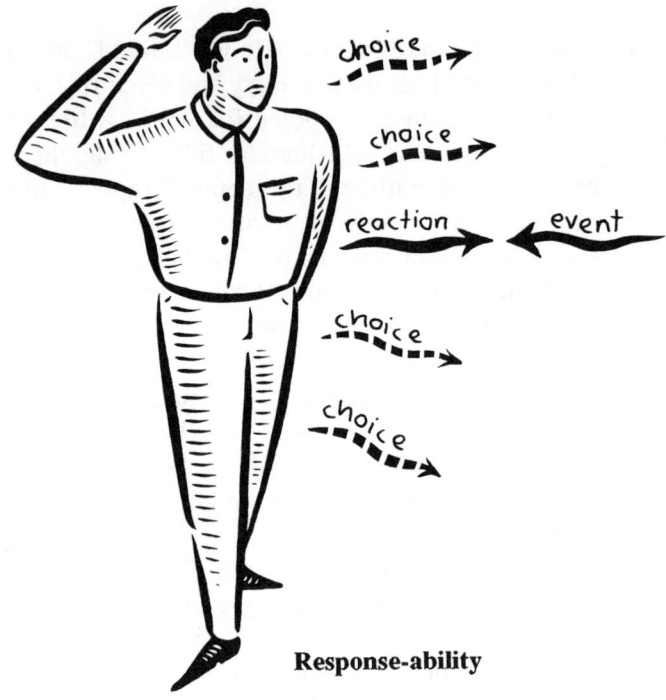

Response-ability

Now, you may think that is a grandiose claim — unlimited joy and freedom! True freedom is, however, what our lives are about if we are "response-able" — so that nothing that occurs on the outside will control the choices and decisions we make. People can fight us, attack us verbally, lie or be unreliable. But when we are personally responsible, we have one face and we stay ourselves, no matter what is happening around us. For instance this is what Victor Frankl, psychologist, discovered in a concentration camp during World War 2. He decided how *he* would be. Nothing that was done to him there made him waver from his determination to retain his humanity and dignity.

"Responsibility" is truly the ability to choose how we want our lives to be. This means not being bound in any way by the past, by a fear of the future, what we were taught, our feelings, our thoughts, our obsessions or pictures. We are in command of our selves. This comes from letting go of our judgements and pictures.

Judith: After being married three times and raising two children, I decided to marry a man twenty years younger than myself. A year after we were married we adopted a three-year-old boy from Cambodia.

To respond in the moment — the present The point of power that contains the greatest opportunity for experience and choice is now, the *present moment*. The moment that something happens it immediately becomes the past as rapidly as it is observed and named. We cannot choose from unlimited options when the moment has passed. We have lost that particular opportunity forever. Living in the moment is like surfing. We have to pay attention or we lose the wave. When we ride the wave, we are being fully alive.

Being in the present is like surfing

The more we are in the "present", the more options we have available to us. Being present includes having full access to all our feelings, intuition, wisdom and common sense. When we are "in reaction" our futures are determined by and will closely mirror our pasts. We just get older.

When we are responsible, we choose to live in the present. We look at each situation as new. We choose to notice when we are "in reaction", in the past, and to feel the underlying feelings to then become present again. We stay vulnerable even when we feel afraid, or angry or hurt. We learn to identify our illusions and projections and judgements and limits. We see bigger and bigger pictures. We create more and more options.

When we are "response-able" we acknowledge that we choose our life from moment to moment, whether we are conscious of it or not. As a consequence, the results that we experience in our lives are not random, spurious or disconnected. We love our inner child and do not treat ourselves as a victim any more. When we are present and not in reaction, we are free to choose our response from *unlimited* options. This is the experience of allowing life to be created by the spontaneity of the moment. We risk new behaviors and create new lives.

Everyone has this opportunity to create personal freedom. There is *nothing* in our past that cannot be healed, no behavior that cannot be changed. We just have to desire it more that we desire to feel comfortable and keep our word even when our inner strength falters.

By truly choosing our response in the present, by responding from pure choice instead of "reaction", we can start a new path, a direct line to our vision. As we move on this path, we *erase the patterning of our past*, and will in the moment begin a new future.

The New Physics discusses time as an illusion and how the past, present and future occur simultaneously. We can experience this theory as fact when we live responsibly.

The source of our experience "Responsibility" also means that we know that *we* are the source of our experience. All experience comes from the self whether we know it or not — the self creates its own experience of whatever is going on. For example, if a friend is abrupt with us, we have unlimited options to respond — for instance we may get hurt, or angry, or concerned about them, or curious about what is going on, or we may smack them on the arm and say "Hey! Remember me!? What's going on?"

How do we learn to become responsible — to live in the present and to truly see ourselves as the sources of our experiences? Let us look again at what we learned in our childhood and see if we can choose new learnings for ourselves now, in the present.

Patterns and feelings Regardless of the situation, we do have the power and the ability to choose how we want to reinterpret our physical sensations to a larger, more abundant point of view. The interpretations we have now are based on the past, from our patterning, and each time we are "in reaction" we choose, albeit unconsciously, to remain in the past. *Every moment is another opportunity.*

Our feelings and thoughts at any moment are the direct result of how we choose to interpret the physical sensations we have from moment to moment. We have this much power in our lives.

Our core experience of any moment is not a feeling but a completely neutral sensation (see Bliss). How we interpret feeling forms our present experience of life.

We can experience the sensation in the present; we are free to reinterpret the sensation into whatever feeling we choose.

Judith: When I was a little girl, my father had a heart attack. Although I do not have a heart condition, sometimes I experience pains in the chest, start sweating and become short of breath. In the past I have immediately become very afraid and have thought I was dying from a heart attack. Now when I experience those sensations I reinterpret them as the feeling of deep grief. I allow myself to feel the grief and just cry and cry. The symptoms go away.

57

We can easily substitute fear and excitement for each other.

EXERCISE: Right now think of something in your life that you are afraid of. See what happens when you switch the sensation from fear to excitement.

The choices we make in one moment determine our feelings and thoughts in the next.

EXERCISE: Next time someone criticizes you, choose to say what is true about the criticism rather than defend yourself.

Being conscious of making choices from moment to moment, day to day, gives us immense ability to choose how we want our lives.

Making the other person the source of our feelings is very common in intimate relationships. It assumes that the other person is in charge of us. To change that experience, to see ourselves as the source of our feelings, requires looking deep within. Rather than "You make me so angry when you come home late and you don't do your share", the true experience could be "I feel angry when you are late. I feel unloved and I want you to do everything you say." It is really okay to ask for exactly what you want, regardless of whether you get it or not.

Being "response-able" means that we can base our behavior on our vision and who we have chosen to be, rather than what we are feeling at the time. We *have* feelings but we *are not* our feelings.

Peg: Choosing to be responsible allowed me to stay in my second marriage. The decision to see myself as the source of how I was feeling, instead of blaming my husband, stayed fuelled by my desire for self-respect. But I so wanted to be right about what I thought was true about him.

But as I kept to my decision, I did begin to see how my interpretations of what was going on had little to do with him. And I began to change my behavior, which kept me from getting what I wanted. For example I complained all the time that he never told me how he saw our relationship. I realized however, that whenever he began to do so, I argued with him. He soon stopped telling me. I then stopped arguing and complaining.

Beliefs The context of "response-ability" means that we create the results in our lives. Seeing ourselves as the source of our feelings is one aspect — how we create our lives from our belief systems is another. As described in Chapter 2, both feelings and beliefs are programed to our past patternings. Our unexperienced feelings and unconscious beliefs run our lives until we choose otherwise.

So how do we become "responsible" for our beliefs? We begin by creating a vision of the person we choose to be. Then we choose the behavior that creates the person. When we act differently than our old patterns, according to our vision, our old belief systems start to show up as resistance (see Chapter 11 The model for change).

It is like flushing a partridge out of the bush. If you just walk by them, they will remain hidden. But if you are close and stop and look for them, they will come flying right out of hiding.

We need to:
• identify the old beliefs that are self-limiting;
• see how our lives have reflected those beliefs;
• accept with compassion that we have chosen them.

When we do that, we are free to choose again, and reprogram ourselves according to a new belief system. Then we can start living accordingly. We achieve that by doing the behaviors that our vision dictates despite our resistance.

Changing a belief or thought without taking the appropriate new action creates an illusion. For example, you may believe: "I'm afraid to talk to people." This belief may stop you from making a phone call that would solve a problem or from creating close friendships. You could choose to live according to the new belief: "Connecting with people brings joy." Talking to people from the new belief creates different results — it will bring you joy! And each time you do it, it will be easier and easier. But if you just think the change without acting it, you will feel crazy, no matter how much you affirm, because you are living in an illusion.

Illusion   An illusion is a state or condition of deceiving one's self. When we live our lives in reaction, we are not being our true selves and we are living in an illusion. The main key to identifying this is learning how to recognize reaction and choosing to leave it behind (see Chapter 4 Reaction).

Projection   To gain the most personal power and knowledge possible about ourselves means we retrieve all instances of projection and blame. We take back all parts of ourselves we have seen as being about others.

> **EXERCISE: List down one side of a page your recollections of when and how you experienced some person or event having done something to you. On the other side of the page, see if you can make it so that you, rather than the event, are the source of your experience. What did you do to make it happen?**

Rape is a frightening and extreme physical and emotional violation. Women who have been raped often blame themselves, withdraw from the world and experience deep guilt, shock and erosion of self-esteem. Let us look at how "responsibility" would work to create personal freedom for a person who has been raped.

"Responsibility" does not mean that when a person is raped, they caused the rape to occur. That is not possible — the rapist did what he did for his own reasons. The likelihood of rape is obviously increased if one walks in a part of town that is known to be dangerous, or if someone has a premonition of danger and ignores it.

How we respond to the rape is the most important part about "responsibility" — how we feel about it, see it, deal with life afterwards, what it does to our future, what assumptions we later make about ourselves, sex and men. Adopting "responsibility", rather than blame or punishment, will completely alter how we experience the event and ourselves.

A woman had been raped at knife-point in Paris when she was on her way to meet her boyfriend. She was in Europe for a two-week holiday while her five-year-old son stayed with her mother. She disappeared for six months after she was raped, and did not contact anybody. She had a violent reaction and did not want people to know. The memories and the repercussions of the rape are still very active. Most of her family and friends still do not know that she was raped or why she disappeared for so long.

She could, however, have got very angry and told the police. She could have told her family and boyfriend how hurt and humiliated she felt, and let them share in the healing of it. She could have used it as an opportunity for incredible intimacy and connection — the very opposite of what the rape had been.

A person who was raped could go after the rapist, as in the movie "The Accused", to find him and do something about it, to choose not to feel so much like a victim. How one responds after the rape determines how that situation is experienced. This way of dealing with the horror of rape applies to any situation where you feel like a victim.

EXERCISE: Remember a situation where you felt like a victim and you even had evidence of the fact. What could you have done to have been more powerful then? What can you do now?

The world of responsibility

The experience of freedom is one of the main benefits of choosing to live response-ably. "Response-ability" allows the freshness and spontaneity of life to create the present rather than the patterned responses of the past. We start to wear one face in the world, where there is no duplicity or separation between what we are now in the moment and what we "should be" or are later on.

"Responsibility" creates self-respect, power and safety inside instead of constantly striving to change the outside to make us feel safe, powerful and okay. We are in charge of our own world. When we consciously choose our beliefs and when we stop blaming and projecting, our self-awareness increases and we open ourselves to more possibilities of love. We feel whole and complete with greater possibilities for new choices based on the last moment and the last moment before that.

The most exquisite result of responsibility is the return home to the sea of bliss, the return to unconditional love.

6
—CHAPTER—
UNCONDITIONAL LOVE

Introduction

Unconditional love is our natural state of being. It is total acceptance of what is. Animals do it — even though they are not aware of it. It is how we are when we are infants, before we start learning to limit, judge and label our life experiences.

Unconditional love

From personal responsibility to unconditional love

Living a life of personal responsibility expands our capacity for experiencing freedom and unconditional love. When we live in the present moment, we experience life's flow as it occurs. Our feelings come and go freely, none better or worse than any other. We put ourselves back into the seat of our personal power. And as we begin to experience how we create our lives from our own beings, we start to feel more full and accepting of ourselves and of others.

This combination of personal responsibility and unconditional love creates bliss, unlimited freedom inside ourselves, and the opportunity to create a life we truly desire.

The key to unconditional love for ourselves and others is to let go of all our judgement — no matter how right or righteous we are!

Judgement

What is judgement? It is making something good or bad or right or wrong. This is different from evaluating a particular situation such as that it is cold outside so we wear boots and a down jacket.

As little children we did not judge until we learned from our families, cultures and environments what "needed" to be judged. Many of the judgements we learned were essential to our survival in our families and as adults we continue to believe the judgements as truths about ourselves, our families and our environments. For instance, snakes and electric outlets are bad — we are not taught the finer distinctions and exceptions! The problem is that when we grow up we keep thinking in the same way, without questioning. We are not as wise as the hedgehog that stopped protecting itself when the outside danger had passed!

We also choose to judge ourselves from what we learn in our culture. From fashion magazines we may, for example, decide we are too fat, too thin, or not fit enough; from a test at school, not intelligent enough; from comparing ourselves with our friends, not good enough or too good. Do not do this or that; this is good, this is bad; do not speak to this person because they are dangerous; this is something you should want; this is right and this is wrong; you should or should not feel this way or that. The list is endless. Judgement is unique to the human mind. Imagine a cat or a dog worrying about the color of their hair or about being fat.

Judgements help define our world and we unconsciously use them to keep our perception of ourselves and the world intact. We use judgements unconsciously to keep ourselves within the boundaries and safety of our childhood. It is the unconscious value that creates problems.

Take the example of prejudice. We may have been conditioned from childhood to believe that we are better or worse than another because of our culture, religion, social class or skin color. The judgement is activated each time we think about or meet someone with whom we compare ourselves, favourably or otherwise. It could stop us from getting to know the person or buying a house in a certain neighborhood — generally it will set up a barrier between ourselves and the other person. The judgement guarantees that we act according to what we originally learned. It will probably also stop us from having our real feelings when we are around that person — because we may like them! A conflict may arise if we are conscious of both our prejudice and our liking at the same time.

EXERCISE: Make a list of your most familiar judgements about:
- **your personality;**
- **your body;**
- **yourself in relationships;**
- **your ability to succeed in business;**
- **your family;**
- **your wife or husband;**
- **your children;**
- **your co-workers;**
- **your childhood;**
- **your country;**

- **your ethnic background;**
- **your color.**

We only judge when we are in reaction — when we are not judging we can make a clear assessment of someone's behavior, performance or intention. When we judge others as better or worse than us, or assign a good or bad value to something about them, we are really projecting and dealing with something about *ourselves*.

For instance we may observe that our partner does not talk much — we are judging them as soon as we assign the value of good or bad to that observation. What do you think that we are judging in ourselves? This part is hard for people to accept but it is one of the most powerful realizations we can make.

We only judge what we see in ourselves. If we accept that as true — it changes our lives. Our judgements are our most serious block to living in unconditional love.

The judgements of "right" and "wrong", which stem from our childhood, are particularly powerful.

How seriously we choose to take our judgements will determine what we experience.

One choice, however, is not better than any other; it will simply lead to different results. A choice to judge a particular race or religion will limit the responsibilities of your relationship with a person of that race or religion. A choice to give up that judgement could lead to wonderful friendships and opportunities that were not possible before.

When we believe that our judgements are the absolute truth about reality, we will not experience what is out there. Our judgements serve as a fence, a barrier that guarantees we will not feel. When we let go of judgement, a flood of experience flows through us and we grow. Judgements block our ability to learn; they cut us off from the full richness of our emotional experience, from our unconditional love. We can release them by simply choosing not to believe them any longer. The thoughts may still be there for a while but even they will fade if we do not pay attention to them.

EXERCISE: If you stopped judging your body, your relationships and so on, what would be true instead? How would you feel?

If we continued our growth without judgement, we would experience our lives with total freedom all the time.

Releasing our judgements will increase our love for ourselves and others, will dissolve our internal barriers, enliven our emotions, brighten the highs, soften and deepen the lows, will fill in the colors of the rainbow, and invite the essence of unconditional love .

From love to unconditional love

Loving allows our creative expression of life. We can give and receive with dignity and compassion. It is holding no judgements and condemning no one.

In this way the feeling of love leads into the state of being of unconditional love. Since we are surrounded by unconditional love already, it is a matter of choosing it — of diving into the sea of bliss. Unconditional love results in clear messages from the heart, powerful loving relationships, success in our work and a joyful life.

The essence of unconditional love is reached by accepting ourselves without judgement.

PART

RELATIONSHIPS

3

Part 3 talks about how our patterning has affected our relationships with our children, lovers and co-workers and how to recognize the pitfalls of those old patterns: *control* and false intimacy.
It talks about how to apply the principles of personal responsibility and unconditional love to all those relationships in order
to create *connection* and *intimacy*. It also talks about our relationship with our own *bodies*, the separation our patterns have created
and how to heal that separation.

7
━━ C H A P T E R ━━
CONTROL

The following chapters on control and intimacy deal with applying the information we have about ourselves.

What is control?

Many people think that control is about telling a child that they have to go to bed, pick up their clothes or be quiet, telling someone what you want them to do or telling an employee what you expect. That is not control. That is being clear and setting limits.

Control is trying to get someone or something to be a certain way without being direct so that *we* do not have to experience *our* uncomfortable feelings.

If for instance, a mother wants a child to stop making a noise she would simply say "Be quiet" or "Play outside". But if the mother is controlling and wants quiet without risking the child's anger she might say "Don't you want to play something quieter now?" or "Mummy's head hurts, dear." Or if a woman wants a man to do something for her, she could ask for exactly that and see if she gets it. If she is controlling, however, she might act helpless so that he feels compelled to assist. Similarly a boss can co-operate with the employees to solve a problem — whereas a controlling boss may unilaterally create a policy and expect it to be obeyed automatically without discussion, threatening the employees with losing their jobs if they do not.

Control comes in many disguises — some more subtle than others. Sometimes it looks like force and threat — that someone can *make* us do something, or that we *have* to do something, that we are under the power of another human or they are under ours.

Control can look very pretty and soft. It can appear wimpy and frightened. Our family history has a lot to do with how good we are at recognizing it — generally we are unable to spot it if it is similar to how we experienced it as a child. If for instance, a man's mother controlled the family by being soft and sweet, he will be unable to recognize control if the woman he is with is controlling in the same way.

"Control" is not the same as power. It is not possible to have control over anything or anybody unless they give it to us. It is not possible to change anything or anybody against their will, no matter how much we may want to. This does not include cases of violent crime such as being held at gunpoint.

We can control ourselves. We control ourselves whenever we change our own experience of something because of our judgements or our choice not to be responsible for how we feel or what we did. For example a parent may be angry at a child and have a *thought* of striking him or her. If the parent judges that thought and thinks that they should always be patient and kind, they will stifle the feeling of anger and erase the thought. Yet they will feel guilty about having it in the first place. The stifled feeling, however, leaks out in other ways. Violence, for example, can be a result of controlling anger. The anger builds and builds and then explodes. Addiction to drugs or alcohol is another result of controlling anger. In that way the drugs numb the anger into chronic pain.

We also control ourselves when we act in ways calculated to gain others' approval.

Peg: Most of my life I wanted to be seen as a loving person. I believed that a loving person was never angry, jealous, demanding or impatient. So whenever I felt any of those things I would hide them. People saw me as saintly and maternal whereas the truth was that I wanted my way in most things and was angry most of the time. I was caught in a trap of my own making. I would make love with my husband when I did not want to. I would drop what I was doing the very instant my son demanded something from me. I swallowed my resentment and smiled. I was a slave to my desire to be seen as a loving person and enraged at how far I'd go to preserve the image. I didn't really want to BE a loving person, just to be seen that way.

A truly loving person is intimate, shares their real self with their family and friends.

The roots of control

Control is a pattern of behavior in relationships that results from our parents' fear of loss. They worried about our well-being. They wanted us to be a certain way so that we would be safe from harm. In their minds it was for us, to keep us safe. After a while, it became a pattern. There was no malice intended.

Giving a child clear instructions like "Be quiet" is setting limits but being indirect is control. Setting limits creates a happy, peaceful child because they are secure in knowing what is expected of them. Control produces a demanding, whingeing child because they have no clear boundaries. They, in effect, demand that someone else stop them.

When a child reaches adolescence, their patterns become set either into rebellion or compliance. So a child who has been controlled to be good and quiet all their life will become a teenager who will usually be either obnoxiously loud and messy, a veritable slug, or turn into a closed and protected, passive goody-goody.

As an adult, the rebel will continue to rebel and will control others so that they rebel too. The goody-goody will want everyone else to be one too. In relationships, the rebel will be loud, messy and demanding whereas the goody-goody will be rigid, up-tight and want their own way. These patterns of relating extend to our work, our pleasure, and all aspects of our lives. Although both patterns appear very different, they come from the same core of being a controlled child.

The results of control

Have you ever tried to change someone? Have you ever tried to change the way someone dresses, for instance, by leaving fashion

magazines where they will see them? Or pinning up advertise-
ments for new clothes? Or have you tried to get someone to lose
weight by putting "Back off Porky" on the refrigerator? Has it
ever truly worked?

Controlling someone to make them different creates anger and
separation. It is lonely to try to change people — it makes you
feel crazy and does not work. Control saps our power. Many
people resist by being very dense when you attempt to control
them, or they act polite, reserved, and confused, or angry and
sneaky. No matter what their particular style of not being controlled, no one was really changed by anyone else.

**EXERCISE: List all the people you have tried to change
or are currently trying to change. How have you tried to
change them? What is/was your most creative way?
How successful have you been? How did you feel about
yourself and the other person afterwards?**

Sometimes people will pretend to change so you will like them,
but people do not really do anything until they decide to. It has
nothing to do with you. Sometimes, in fact, trying to get someone
to do something has the opposite effect because anyone who was
controlled as a child will most likely respond by rebelling as an
adult.

Even if it is something they really want, most people will fight
you if you tell them they have to do it. For example a boss wanted
his employees not to speak to each other on the job because he
believed that this interfered with productivity. So he instituted a
"no visiting" rule. Employees could have lost their jobs for not
following it. Of course everyone rebelled! They still visited each
other but only when the boss was not around. And productivity
suffered.

How was the "no visiting" rule control? The boss tried to regu-
late the employees' social behavior, not their job performance.

What he really wanted was for his company to be successful
and for the employees to participate in that success. He was also
worried about profits. So to get the results he wanted he could
have let them know that the profit margin was deteriorating and

then asked them for their input, since they had the first-hand information about what was or was not working.

There used to be a very clear separation between our work life and home life and we wanted to keep them separate. We know now that separation could not work — that separation was an illusion. We are one person and if we attempt to keep our lives in compartments and segments, we end up feeling desperate, lonely and in many cases alienated from ourselves.

In work situations, employees whose input is valued, who are given clear guidelines for job performance and then expected to be responsible for their results are an asset to any company. Employees who are controlled behave like children or will probably have to leave their jobs.

We learned to control ourselves as children because we were afraid of losing our parents' love. We wanted them so much. We would do anything to have them. We then try to control our own children out of our desire that they love us and to keep them safe. We try to control ourselves in our relationships and control the people we love so that they will continue to want us. We try to control our employees out of a fear of what will happen to our businesses if we do not, or we try to control our bosses out of a fear of what will happen to our jobs. We are so afraid of loss that we create that loss by not experiencing our fear and by not trusting ourselves.

Control comes from a fear of loss.

Control = fear of loss

Think of what you are afraid to lose and how you try to control it. Control tends to increase fear because it creates separation and anger.

> **EXERCISE: Think about the parent who controlled you. How did you feel then? How do you feel now? For the next ten minutes sit quietly and notice how you try to control what you are doing, thinking and feeling.**
>
> **For tomorrow, keep a journal of how you are tempted to change yourself or any experience you or another person is having. Then ask yourself what you feared losing? Notice how often you allowed the fear to determine your behavior.**

Taking care of

Not wanting to feel certain feelings also creates a very subtle type of control called "taking care of". "Taking care of" people has nothing to do with being a useful human — physically helping others, taking out the garbage, offering your seat on the bus to an elderly person, buying your partner their favorite food at the supermarket and so on.

"Taking care of" is the act of trying to stop, change or create a particular experience for someone else rather than experiencing how you feel when you are around them. For instance, when a person is crying and someone goes to comfort them without being asked, usually the person crying *has to* stop, not because they feel "helped" but to curtail the other person's "taking care of" behavior. They feel obliged to stop crying because that person is giving them a tissue or patting them on the back or hugging them — they have to do something to get the other person to leave them alone. So what really happens is that when we try to stop someone from feeling bad or sad, that person has to stop what they are experiencing so that we will leave them alone. It is like a boomerang.

> **EXERCISE: Remember how you do that with people you love and how they do that with you.**

Taking care of someone else is a way to control their feelings so that we will not feel so uncomfortable in the presence of their strong feelings.

Taking care of = controlling someone's feelings

When you "take care of", you will feel disrespectful, resentful, superior or entitled. So will the person you are trying to take care of.

Control as parents

All our judgements about ourselves and how we behave to avoid discomfort erupt like a bad dream when we become parents.

What we often do with our children to stop them from acting a certain way can backfire because it stops us from assuming our responsibility of teaching them to be personally responsible. Instead that control promotes a demanding child who anticipates getting what they want by being demanding.

For example if your child wants a toy when you are in a toy store, you may feel compelled to give your child whatever they want out of feeling inadequate as a parent, or for fear of having a scene in public if you say "no". If you buy the toy to shut up the child, you are controlling yourself and your child. And it denies the child the experience of learning what it feels like to be told "no".

Peg: I had my youngest child when I was thirty-seven and my other two sons were thirteen and seventeen. I focused all my attention on the youngest, giving him everything he wanted. He had more toys than any other child in recorded history. I wanted him to see me as the most wonderful person in the world. He became more and more demanding — he had no choice. It was how I trained him to be. We were both so relieved when I finally started to say "no" to him.

Giving a child everything he wants turns him into a pig

It is important to allow our children to feel everything, because they do anyway! It is just that the feeling, if we try to stop it, goes underground. So they have to consciously learn how to deny the experience even though they still have the feeling. This creates a reaction in the child, the beginning of a lie, a pretence. The child will start learning that it is not okay to have the full experience of themselves and begin the process of separation from reality.

We all have a right to our full experience of ourselves.

EXERCISE: Here is a simple exercise to discover whether you are controlling yourself or your child:
You and your child are in a toy store shopping for a birthday gift for a party the child is going to. You have already told your child that you are not buying anything for him/her. You are then asked to get them a toy that they have just found, that they have been looking for, for months.
1   You say "What did Mummy tell you before we came? Didn't you promise not to ask for anything?"
2   You get it for them anyway because they have been looking for it for so long.
3   You buy it and make them promise not to ask for anything else for a month.
4   You say "no" and let them feel whatever they feel.
If you answered any but (4) it is likely that you do not want to be responsible for setting *clear and consistent* limits with your child but are controlling both of you in order to avoid discomfort.

Here is a sure-fire way to know that you are controlling: are you trying to change anything in any way so that you will not have to feel what you are feeling?

How to give up control

If your answer to the question above is "yes", do not be surprised. Most people want to control other people. It is rare to be with someone who does not want to control.

Control is not a feeling but a compulsion.

It comes from feeling out of control, feeling insignificant and having a fear of loss. Usually when we try to control, we are feeling inadequate, and a lot of the time it is unconscious.

No one can ever control you.

On the other hand, if you find yourself fighting against control, it is a clear indication that you are seeking to control someone or something at that point — possibly yourself, as in not telling that person to shut up. If you had no interest in control, someone could do something of a controlling nature and you would look at them and say to yourself, "Isn't that interesting?" and completely ignore it. It would not affect you in any way.

If you want to give up control, you need to re-program yourself — to re-parent the child in you who is afraid of loss. You need to teach that child that it is okay to feel everything, think everything and to know what is true. And besides that, you must no longer let that child's past needs determine *your* behavior now. You would not allow a five-year-old child to determine how you will be now. Why would you let your inner child do it?

Remember the child in the toy store? You need to set limits on the child that was you as well. Let him or her throw a fit inside you about not getting their way, but *you* decide what you are going to do and who you are going to be. It is not that difficult to do once you have chosen. If you do that, no one will be able to control you because you will not be predictable in your response. You will not be in reaction. You will be present.

Choose how you are going to be in every situation. Do not let anyone's style, energy, success or anything stop you from being exactly how you have chosen to be. Control will no longer be a factor in your life.

When you do that you will be in control of your life. Your choice will be law in your universe, not your feelings. This results in tremendous self-esteem and equality.

EXERCISE: How do you usually respond when some-one is angry, demanding, loving or sexual and the feel-ing is directed at you? How do you want to respond? What control will you need to let go of to achieve this response?

Equality

"Equal" means "having the same value." It does not mean "similar" or "the same as". Between humans, behaving as equals gives us the freedom to share ourselves as we are. It also means that we view everyone as the source of their own experience, that we are all equally capable of creating our life's experience and making choices — even if we are not always conscious of those choices.

Now this does not make any sense when we immediately think of all the people who are clearly the victims of oppressors, or children born with serious disease to drug-addicted parents. Yet, although we are not saying that people are born into equally healthy environments, we are saying that all humans are capable of deciding how to interpret their day-to-day experience. And the way we interpret life's events can determine the outcome of the situation.

Judith: Our friend Jill developed breast cancer and she used that experience of disease to revamp her life — to stop many behaviors that robbed her of her personal power. She has just had reconstructive breast surgery and is now a partner in a successful company that she created since her cancer.

We often have a hard time accepting that the choices others make are as equal as are our own, or understanding why they choose what they do. But how are we to really know what motivates another person or what they value? Because someone has chosen differently to ourselves, it does not mean that they are not worthy of our respect.

EXERCISE: Bring to mind the people you have known who have chosen life-styles you judge. What thoughts do you have to change in order to see their choice as equal to what you would have chosen for them.

Seeing and behaving towards another human as equal, regardless of age or circumstance, will create respect and joy.

8

━ C H A P T E R ━

INTIMACY AND CONNECTION

Even though we may no longer consciously know it, we are all connected. There is no separation.

Most of us have memories of being little, loved and held by our parents and people who cared about us, even if it happened just for moments at a time. Those memories, even if they are only experienced as a yearning in our bodies, draw us into relationship after relationship, searching for that memory to become a reality again. Intimacy allows us to feel close to whomever we choose, whenever we want. It allows us to choose how we will behave in every relationship.

Imagine being with someone and feeling open and loving and connected. You shared your feelings and thoughts without guile. You did not hide. You did not feel the need to protect yourself around them. And maybe they shared what they felt and what they thought, and maybe they did not. However, you feel wonderful, because you are sharing. You chose intimacy and that choice feels good.

Maybe later that evening or the next day you become uncomfortable about what you said or the way you said it. You start to wonder what they think about you. You might even imagine that they judge you for being so open, for saying so many personal things about yourself. Then you begin to judge yourself. You react to being so vulnerable, so intimate. You start to close up and protect yourself, and the next time you see that person you act as if that connected, open moment had never happened.

We all have that choice in our relationships: whether to be intimate and move deeper inside or to protect ourselves and stay in the illusion of aloneness.

What is intimacy and connection?

Most of us think we are being intimate when we talk about how the other person makes us feel. And in the midst of our strong feelings, this is really easy to do and reflects the world of our beliefs.

Intimacy, however, is talking to somebody about what is true about ourselves, and being responsible when we do it.

Intimacy means saying how you feel and what you want — about anything. It does not mean the other person has to do what you want either. But it gives them information about you and gives them you.

Peg: Sometimes I feel too loved by my husband, too wanted. It makes me uneasy, I'm afraid to be that happy. If I choose to be intimate I say all that to him. And then I feel safer feeling his love. If I choose protection, I will just withdraw or say something to push him away so he'll stop being so loving. When I do that I feel more comfortable momentarily but I feel lonely and unhappy too. I'm protected. And it costs me a lot.

Intimacy also means hearing what the other person feels and wants, not just listening to their words. It means hearing the intention of their communication, not interpreting their words or taking things literally when you know what they mean. In other words it means your giving up being right and, most importantly, a willingness to receive them.

Peg: I can remember fighting with my husband and not hearing anything he really said. In fact, I can remember taking his words and changing them inside my head. And then responding to him from the changes I made in my head, not what he said or meant. I was too afraid to be that close, to give up my point of view. I needed to be right. If I responded to what he was really saying, I would have felt too vulnerable about my past decisions and I didn't want to experience that in front of anybody, not even myself.

How to be intimate

Imagine that you are listening to the following conversation; notice how you feel as the conversation progresses.

J: I feel that you're a selfish person.

P: Oh, yeah? Well I feel that you're a selfish person.

J: You're interrupting me. Let me talk.

P: You know you never, ever, ever just let me say what's going on!

Do you recognize that? It is not intimacy. When we say the words, "I feel", then we are being intimate. But watch out — after "I feel", you could say anything!

Here is the way Judith would say it if she were being responsible and intimate.

J: You know I can't stand the way I feel when I want something from you and you won't give it to me.

(Do you feel the difference so far?)

J: You know I want your attention. I love to get your attention and I feel as if I don't have attention when I'm around you. I feel like I'm back with my mother and father and I can't stand how I feel.

Now Judith is only talking about Judith. So Peg may say something like:

P: You know, I'm really uncomfortable showing you how I feel. I get really afraid about how much I love you so I pretend that I don't want you.

Now, the last exchange is really a far cry from Judith saying to Peg, "I think you're selfish."

To create intimacy, you speak about you and only you.

It is not conceited or selfish. It is really the opposite. It is the most loving way we can be with someone. We can think about intimacy as meaning

"into-me-see".

We require some new learning and constant practice and commitment. We need to be willing to make lots and lots of mistakes.

And then to make more mistakes. When we are committed to living our purpose, our mistakes are just moments of opportunity. Look at the following statements and see how they can be made either intimate or non-intimate.

I feel angry when you touch me, because...
Non-intimate: I think you're a rotten lover.
Intimate: I feel angry when I'm touched. Or, I feel so afraid to feel vulnerable that I can barely stand it.

I feel sick being around you, because...
Non-intimate: I think you're weak. You always seem to want me to do things for you without saying what they are.
Intimate: I would like to control you to take better care of yourself so I don't have to feel so uncomfortable when you don't.

I'm in love with you, because...
Non-intimate: You're so warm and tender.
Intimate: I love how tender I feel toward you.

I think you're so interesting...
Non-intimate: You've done so many interesting things that I haven't.
Intimate: I'd like to get to know you better and I'm afraid you won't like me if I let you see me.

I hate it when you're late, because...
Non-intimate: I think you're irresponsible and selfish to keep me waiting.
Intimate: I feel hurt because I think you don't care about our relationship.

I'm sad that you don't want me any more, because...
Non-intimate: You are much more open than you used to be.
Intimate: I feel terrible about how many times I pushed you away.

You're always saying that about me and I wish you'd stop it, because...
Non-intimate: I'm sick of you hurting my feelings.
Intimate: My feelings get hurt. But really it's because I know that what you are saying is true — I'm beginning to see how I push people away. I don't want to do that any more and at the same time I'm afraid to change in case I lose myself.

In the late 1970s and early 1980s people were starting to learn the formula for intimacy. People were taught to "actively listen" and to make "I" sentences. The problem was that people would just take the formula and keep blaming people. People would say, "I feel that you hurt me. I feel that you won't let me share myself." See how this blames the other person for how we are feeling inside?

The results are very different when we just talk about ourselves. When we do that, the other person's response usually contains a feeling of openness. There is an experience of love or of being loved, no matter what the content is that we are sharing. Even if we are saying, "I hate the way I feel about me right now, or, I love you with all my heart."

This is because when we say what is true about us, and we are talking only about us, we are truly sharing.

When we share, we connect.

Sometimes it happens that the connection feels scary to the person we are talking to, and they react by closing up.

Even if the other person closes up we need to continue being intimate. For then we are rewarded by feelings of strength, self-respect and clarity. Too often we allow ourselves to be guided by the other person's responses and we give up our integrity and intimacy and choose protection.

Intimacy happens by pure choice. It is not easy for anyone at first to take responsibility for how they feel. Intimacy happens when you really know that no matter what your thoughts, you are the source of your feelings. In the middle of a sentence, you may change your words to more responsible ones. You will be different to be with. You may be very uncomfortable in the beginning. You may sound funny or unusual. You may feel stilted. And the desire to blame somebody else may be really strong at first. It may be so strong that you will have to get some sticky tape for your mouth and some babysitters for your mind.

Intimacy can feel so good that we start to feel wonderful about ourselves. And although it does not make sense, it is at this moment that our deepest negative thoughts about ourselves bubble to the surface. You see, they are brought to our consciousness by the sharing of love. They become challenged. We feel jolted out of our familiar state and we go into paradox. Our new feelings flood in to mix with our past experience. It feels like oil and water. Even though this experience can feel terrible, it is our window to intimacy. It is a moment that can open our hearts to love.

The benefits of intimacy

Connection is the result of intimacy. We all need to experience connection. We shrivel up inside without it and when we are intimate, other people become attracted and want to be with us.

We feel so good about ourselves and judging stops.

Into-me-see

Intimacy is the underlying principle of all powerful, joyful and vibrant relationships. A lot of people think it means sex. It does not but it can certainly make you feel like making love. And when we make love intimately, it is quite a different experience than making love from a physical desire without the intimacy. When we are intimate and make love, we experience deep connection and bonding and we merge. All we really want in relationships is to be close and connected. If we have that, we have all the safety we need to grow and be fulfilled in our lives. And once we choose to live intimately and we risk our protection, we discover we did not need that protection anyway.

So why be intimate? The more you let yourself feel and know what is going on inside you the more powerful you can be in your relationships with your lover, friend, family or co-workers. The deepest intimacy you can experience is to say whatever it is that you are experiencing, like a small child. It is to say, "I don't want to make love right now" in the moment, without adding anything or taking anything away. Even if you think you will die, just say it. You are vulnerable when you are intimate. why would you want to risk that? Because the pay-off is so good: people are drawn to you; they open up; you feel safer than when you are protecting yourself; you see and feel more; the world is a bigger place.

When you are not saying what is going on inside you, when you are not sharing, your perception dulls. Things get denser. The plumbing starts to clog up, you get fat and depressed and create a heavy atmosphere. Some people think that it is not a good idea to say what is really going on because it can get them into trouble. It is true that the person you share yourself with can become upset or hurt and then you might feel guilty or upset too! But what is wrong with upsets? Do they not allow an opportunity to grow and create new options? Not being intimate is a great way to control yourself and your growth.

Being careful with someone, pretending, withholding or lying builds walls inside you, around how you feel about that person. Your life may seem peaceful but it will probably be dull, unhappy and lonely.

Carried to an extreme, those walls can turn into a fort and result in long-term separation from someone you love.

Peg: My father had a fight with his only living brother when I was a child. They stopped speaking — for thirty years. My father was hurt and wanted his brother to come to him to apologise. It's too late now, my uncle died last year. Now my father wishes he had gone to him to talk about it. But he was not used to talking about hurt feelings or even realizing that he was hurt, and the habit of a lifetime won. There's an emptiness in him where his brother's love belongs.

EXERCISE: Right now, tell yourself something about you that you have kept secret from childhood. Why have you kept it a secret? How has this secret affected your relationships with the people you love?
You now have the power to tell someone else that secret. And it does not matter what they think of it. It only matters that you are able to share it. Tell that secret to someone in person or by phone, and tell them how you feel about telling them. Will you do it now or will you do it later?

Doing this exercise lets you know that you are the source of how you feel. This is personal responsibility and is the perspective that will create intimacy and connection in all your relationships.

9
— CHAPTER —
BODIES

Bodies! Bodies! Bodies!

We worry about AIDS, cancer, cholesterol, fat, varicose veins, baldness, constipation, insomnia, colds, heart attacks, cellulite, sagging breasts, grey hair, hemorrhoids, body odor and so much more. Most of us are more concerned with how our bodies look than how we treat them. Or we are obsessed with our health and treat our bodies like they are all we are!

We eat and drink unconsciously and diet and exercise mercilessly. We become drug and sex addicts. We are compelled to try to make our bodies fit some outside standard of fitness and beauty.

How do our bodies look?

90

We forget that when we were children, we stayed fit and healthy by continually using our bodies to play. We ate when we were hungry if we could get away with it and wore what was comfortable and what we liked. The focus on bodies and the need to be attractive has flooded the media and our minds over the past thirty years. This consciousness has propelled us into our separating ourselves from our feelings and our bodies.

Our body is a finely tuned instrument that shows us at every moment how well we are living our lives. Our bodies are the sacred home of our souls.

How we look and how we feel about how we look gives us instant feedback about our beliefs and how well they are serving us. Our body's ability to feel all feelings, experience joyful and fulfilling sex, and our willingness to give and receive love are indicators of our true health.

How our bodies reflect us

When we are little, our bodies are supple and firm. We can do anything we want with them, from throwing a ball, running and hiking, tap and ballet dancing to really relaxing. We can teach our bodies almost anything. And they always remember what we teach them. Once we learn how to ride a bike, our bodies remember that into our adulthood. They also remember how to feel and be healthy. Yet our experience of life in our childhood and our interpretations of our parents' points of view also have an effect on our bodies that can last for the rest of our lives.

When we began wanting our parents' approval, we forgot that our bodies belonged to us and were our chief vehicle for enjoying life. We became separated from our bodies! We began to mistrust them or their capabilities.

So now we do not listen to them enough about what feels good, what they need to eat, how much exercise they need, what their unique natural shapes are. Instead we look to others to tell us how to be in our bodies, what we should eat, how we should look. Or we become numb to them and ignore them entirely: eating or starving in order to stay numb, never exercising, drinking too much alcohol, doing whatever we can just to dull our experience of separation.

Food and eating

Many of our eating habits come from the pattern of how we were fed as infants. When we were babies and experienced the physical sensation of hunger, we cried. If we were fed, all was well. But say that our mother could not stand to hear a baby crying. She would feed us whenever we were hungry, or whether we were hungry or not. So we cried harder. The sensation of hunger was now transformed into a feeling of upset — the very thing she was trying to control. If, on the other hand, our mothers felt inadequate when we were hungry and we cried, she would treat us in ways that eventually taught us that crying was not okay. The sensation of hunger was expressed in a way that was not okay with her. Later on we may unconsciously think that it is the sensation of hunger that is not okay and it may be very difficult or unusual for us to experience real hunger.

Judith: When I was born I was breast-fed for two or three weeks. My mother stopped breast-feeding because there wasn't enough milk, so I stopped feeling hungry. I had no desire to eat and I was fed through an eye-dropper at night when I was asleep. In fact my mother spent a lot of her time when I was an infant making food that she could then puree so that I could eat. Food was a big deal.

When I was a teenager and began to experience teenage crises, I reacted through food. I would either eat and vomit, not eat and become anorexic, or think about food all day long. And that way of handling crises came from the pattern of how I was fed when I was an infant. To keep me alive and because I was angry as an infant, eating (and not eating) was a forced event from the beginning — one that demanded extra attention. For me, force became a part of eating from early infancy.

Peg: When I was very young, meal-times were wonderful. I would climb out of my high-chair and into my father's lap where I would sit enthroned for the rest of the meal. I adored him.

As I grew older, meal-times in my family became the arena for my parents' cold war in an increasingly painful relationship. I became withdrawn and ate more and more as a substitute for comfort. As their relationship deteriorated, meals were silent and tense. They divorced when I was seventeen. I was relieved and heartbroken. But I stopped being hungry.

By the time I was nineteen, I weighed ninety pounds (about forty kilograms). It was a time when I didn't want to have any feelings at all, and eating became the same thing as feeling. And so if I could just not eat, and not notice that I wasn't eating, then I wouldn't have to feel. Later, whenever there was a time of intense feelings that were not okay in my history of beliefs, one of the things that I would unconsciously do was to stop eating so that I wouldn't have to feel.

EXERCISE: Our basic eating patterns determine how we eat, what we eat, when we eat and how we think about food now. To discover some of your patterns, start to look at how you deal with food.
1   **What are your favorite foods?**
2   **When did you first eat them?**
3   **How were they presented to you?**
4   **What is it like now?**
5   **In what way would your life be different if you ate only what you were hungry for and when you were really hungry?**
Spend a week eating only what and when you really want to. What feelings and memories surface? If you keep to this exercise no matter what your experience, you will begin to repattern your relationship with eating. It will heal your inner child.

Disease

It is our opinion that some disease may well begin with a thought. The thought, repeated often enough, solidifies into a belief. The belief suppresses certain emotional experiences. The suppressed feelings collect inside us as matter, and may then create disease. The last stage of disease is when it affects the body. So most serious disease takes a long time to develop. A disease of the body can have an emotional component, and a belief component.

A woman we will call Blanche never felt "quite good enough". She grew up in a very religious family that saw sex and marriage as a requirement of each other. She rebelled and had a series of love affairs as a young woman. In her late twenties, never having become pregnant, she decided to "experiment" to see if she could. She intended to get an abortion if she did. Well, she could, and she did have the abortion. She didn't feel anything.

In her early thirties she married a very good, loving man. She judged her past and hid most of it from her husband. She got pregnant and three months later was diagnosed as having cancer. She was advised to get rid of the baby in order to save her life, but decided not to. When the baby was one-and-a-half she finally told her husband about the abortion, shared with him how awful she felt about it, and discovered that he loved her anyway.

At that time she was about to start some very expensive cancer treatment but decided not to. She died three days later. Her husband reported that those last three days were the most intimate they had ever shared — her guilt was gone. If she had stopped judging herself and had just felt her feelings, she might never have developed the cancer.

Fitness and exercise

How we treat our bodies is also a pattern learned from childhood — for instance, whether we can trust our bodies to heal themselves or whether we have to always be on guard against germs or constipation; whether our bodies are a source of pleasure or of sin; whether we are athletes or couch potatoes.

Judith: I was eight years old and on the gymnastics team at school. I had just learned how to stand on my head and do somersaults. When I came home to show my parents what I had learned, my father panicked. He told me never to stand on my head; that I would break my neck. I quit the team the following week. I became very afraid of hurting myself and stopped trusting my body for many years. It wasn't until I was forty years old that I started being physical again. It has taken me many years to deal

94

with my fear and my belief that my father was right — that I would break my neck.

EXERCISE: Now would be a very good time for you to close the book and your eyes and allow yourself to drift back to a time in your childhood when you were free with your body. Remember the physicality of childhood and what you did for fun. Remember running and sledding and skiing and swimming. Remember anything that was pleasurable to you. Allow at least ten minutes to remember and re-experience the freedom you felt in your body. Now ask yourself, "What happened? What decisions did I make that limited my body freedom? How do I feel about those decisions? Do I want to make new ones? What are they?"

This separation from our bodies can end. We can reconnect our minds and our bodies, learn to trust our bodies again and to treat them with respect. Our bodies will faithfully reflect the choices we make — no matter what those choices are.

Judith: I decided to learn how to ski. I was very afraid of losing control so every time I would go down a trail, I would hear my father's voice telling me I was going to break my neck again. My inner child was in terror. She could barely stay breathing.

A friend decided to help me get over my fear. We went up a lift in Aspen, Colorado, and I cried all the way up, sharing my fear the whole way. After we reached the top of the lift and skied to the apex, he turned backwards, smiled and said, "Follow me". He began to ski down the mountain backwards, very slowly. I felt my fear drain away, return and drain away again as I followed him face forwards and reparented that inner child as I went.

I also had the direct experience of my father laughing. He has been dead for over five years. I know he approved.

If we choose to love our bodies and live in them instead of outside of them, looking critically at them; if we feed them healthy foods, take pleasure in the way they can move and play — our bodies will eagerly respond.

95

Happy bodies

EXERCISE: What are your beliefs about your body? Stand naked in front of a mirror and notice whether you are willing to love every part of your body. If not, commit yourself to accepting each part of your body and you will be free to change it.

Sexuality

We had a full range of feelings when we were little. Some were alright and some were not. Our expression of sexual feelings was probably tempered by our parents' discomfort with their sexual feelings, together with society's mores. We usually interpreted their discomfort with a belief that our bodies were not okay or that sexuality was not okay.

When we were very small our sexuality was diffused in that we experienced sensations all over that were sensual and erotic and warm. In fact, during birth itself both the mother and the infant experience a combination of feelings that range from sexual and ecstatic to painful and terrifying. This trip through the birth canal is the child's first sensual experience and has a great deal to do with his or her future sexuality.

When we became toddlers and young children we were taught to sublimate or hide our sexuality.

Judith: I remember hiding in our basement with my best friend when I was no more than five years old. We explored each other's bodies, while I made sure my parents were not coming down the steps. When I was a teenager I kept watching out whenever I was making out with anyone. And now, as a grown woman I still look around to make sure my parents are not watching.

Most of us did what we were told — or versions of it — and by doing that we began our separation from our sexuality. That is not an indictment of our history. That was the best our parents could teach us with the information they had to go on. And we also did the best we could.

Perversions

Sexual feelings are normal and are not such a big deal. If we had been trained to allow our feelings, to be able to feel sexual, or angry or sad or joyful and not hide it or act it out, we would probably not have rape, passionless violence or substance abuse as problems in our world. Now, that sounds very simplistic to most of us, yet think about it for a while. What is your opinion?

You see, when we can contain our feelings in our bodies, and not be afraid of them or feel compelled to act them out or even share them, we are free. When we become responsible for our bodies and our experiences of life,

97

our sexual feelings are as normal and welcomed as being hungry.

Most people who commit rape or any act of violence are not able to experience their sexuality or their anger without "acting it out" and they become so frightened of the experience they are having that they focus it on someone else. In fact, they think the other person has done something that has caused the act to occur.

EXERCISE: Remember a time when you felt so sexual you became afraid that you might do something you would be sorry for later. This time, let yourself feel that sexuality for ten minutes. When thoughts come into your mind, thank them and ask them to go on their way. Imagine those thoughts like rootless trees — watch them go by. Do not plant them. Just feel your sexuality.

The recipe for ecstatic sex — how to heal your sexuality

In its pureness our sexuality is a source of joy and connectedness. Unfortunately for many of us it is less than that. We judge ourselves as unlovable or inadequate, we make love when we do not truly want to, or do not make love even when we do truly want to. We are afraid to be intimate. So we often just do the physical act of sex and end up feeling lonely afterwards.

The recipe for ecstatic sex

1 Make love only when you really want to. No reason is a good enough reason to have sex except that you want to.
2 Share everything. Tell your partner everything you are feeling during the time you are making love, no matter what fear that may activate.
3 Be responsible for your sexual experience and let the other person be responsible for theirs. No one can turn you on and you cannot turn anybody else on.
4 Laugh. Laughter attracts all the gods from all the worlds, heals disease and keeps us young.

You can heal anything in your sexual history as well, simply by choosing how you are going to experience the event *now*.

Peg: When I was eleven years old I was molested by my next-door neighbor, a man who had no children. For many, many years I kept it a secret, being ashamed of what happened and afraid to risk the punishment I was sure would happen. And I hated that man. My shame and hate affected my ability to feel any sexual feelings as an adult. I have since altered my experience of that event. I now see him as a very lonely, emotionally young person and myself as a frightened, lonely child who did not realize she could have stopped him. He was neither a large nor very powerful man. I could have screamed, fought, run. I was wanting everyone's approval too much to do any of those. I even wanted his approval. I see both of us with compassion now. I can finally feel my body and sexuality as my own.

Heal your past sexuality.

EXERCISE: Spend a day looking around to see who attracts you sexually. Do not do anything about it. Just let yourself enjoy being attracted. Then think about how your family dealt with sexuality. Now imagine that you are a child and you are allowed to feel everything. Watch your body get clearer and clearer inside to allow space for all the feelings. Imagine that you are sharing these feelings with your family and this time they let you feel everything. They feel wonderful. And then go back to the incidents when you were attracted to someone. Do those incidents feel any different now? Are you more comfortable with your feelings?

PART

SUCCESS AND CHANGE

4

This part addresses the how and the why of change. It talks about the *sources of information* we have available to deal with the choices we have to make about change: our head, heart, soul, support, mass consciousness and universal consciousness; and about the importance of each. It speaks about the actual structure of change, how it occurs and what prevents it and a *model* for how to achieve it successfully. And finally, *the big picture* of why change is so important now.

10

━━ E H A P T E R ━━

SOURCES OF INFORMATION

"Mirror, mirror on the wall, who is the fairest one of all?" asks Snow White's wicked and maligned stepmother.

"To be or not to be?" Hamlet asks himself the essential question.

"What, will these hands ne'er be clean!?" pleads Lady Macbeth to the universe.

Who will take me to the ball?" Cinderella waits for someone to take care of her.

Each of these questions is of passionate interest to the individual involved. Most of us find ourselves wrestling with equally weighty issues and making everyday decisions about them. These decisions affect our lives and everyone else's. Where and how do we obtain the best information necessary to make our choices clear? This chapter is about many sources of information available to us.

Information within us

We have three very powerful sources of information within us which we can sum up as: our head, our heart and our soul.

Our "head"

Our "head" is like a computer in our brain. It contains every experience of our past — everything we have ever learned. The data are stored in orderly files ready to access and apply. Our head is programed to respond to incoming stimulation by supplying the appropriate reference file of information. For example we do not need to learn to drive every time we want to use a car because our head has that information stored. Our head is essential for things like that: how to write a check, diaper a baby or do our taxes. It can also access memories and words to songs, put thoughts together to form complex sentences and recreate our multiplication tables. It is our automatic pilot. We would be lost without it.

When it comes to our present relationships, however, our heads are not a useful and dependable source of information. We were programed in our childhood to see things according to our original belief systems and our head continues to do that, even though the situation in the present is not the same. For example if you believed in childhood that being isolated was safer than being vulnerable, your head will interpret overtures of love as a threat. And it will be certain that the threat is real. It does that through its analysis of the situation. Everything is filtered through the same beliefs.

If we live mainly by the information we receive from our heads, and many people from western cultures do, we are likely to to interpret all our new experiences according to our belief systems.

We interpret everything that now happens according to what has already happened. The only experience we can value is one that is acceptable to our heads. It is hard to learn any new information about ourselves because everything has to fit the existing system. It is rare to have a new file open. Operating from our head can limit us to living a monochromatic life.

EXERCISE: For an example of information from your head, ask your head right now why you are reading this book. Look up while you ask the question. (Write down the answer.)

Our "heart"

Another source of information is the "heart". This term has been used metaphorically as the center of human emotions for hundreds of years. The "heart" can be regarded as the source of our experience of what is happening *now*. It is not programed by the past. In fact its information is often wildly different than what our head's information tells us. Our "heart" tells us how we are feeling, what we want, and what we are experiencing right now. It is a moment-by-moment present-time source of information. It is easy to access! To find out what your "heart" has to say, all you need to do is ask it something. At first it helps to focus your attention inward toward your "heart area" when you are asking a question. And *it is critical to accept the first answer you get.* Information from the heart can often be surprising and your head may well want to argue.

For example, our heart may miss a friend and want to ring her up right now. And our head may say, "No, no. It's too late to call her now, she's probably asleep." Our head is operating on the belief that it is safer to see it as wrong to bother people after a certain time of night.

EXERCISE: Let us test our heart's information. Ask your heart why you are reading this book and look down. Take the first answer. Remember what your head said? Are the answers the same?

If you would like more practice in head/heart answers, here is an exercise:

Ask the following questions of both your head and heart; write down the answers you get:

- **Why do you have the job that you do?**
- **What do you most want from the person you are with? Or**
- **Why are you not in a relationship?**
- **What would you most like to change about yourself?**
- **What would make you the happiest?**

Without information from our hearts we would be automatons. We would be robots.

Our soul

Our souls provide us with the deepest source of information about ourselves — our purpose and our core values. It is the backdrop, the stage upon which we design our lives. We become aware of it through our lives in many quiet moments, or whenever we really ask for guidance. Our core values are formed deep in our souls and are directly related to our purpose. Living according to our core values is truly being in integrity and creates joy. Not living according to our core values produces guilt. There is a world of difference between our heart and our soul. Whereas our heart does not recognize when we are in an illusion, but will respond in accordance with that illusion, our soul will always respond in integrity with our core purpose for being here. It would be much easier for us to be willing to commit to living our soul's purpose.

True guilt is a message from our souls to *change our behavior, right now*. Some people call it the "voice of conscience." It comes on its own, whether we are searching our souls about that behavior or not. Whenever we behave in ways that are not in keeping with our core values, we experience true guilt. This does not have anything to do with punishment or shame. In fact, self-punishment will inhibit the message from our awareness. True guilt demands that we immediately correct our behavior so that we have self-respect and stay on course for our purpose. For example whenever we treat a child harshly, lie to a friend or fail to keep our agreements, we will feel guilty. When this guilt occurs, it is a physical sensation. We can depend on it.

False guilt happens in our heads and is about getting caught and being punished. We have it programed in from all the times we

106

were punished as a child for a particular sort of behavior, like using "bad" language.

When we do not listen to *our soul's* message to change our behavior, we lose self-respect. Carried to an extreme, our refusal to correct our behavior turns into self-punishment and the punishment *seems* to atone for not changing our behavior — for example "If I feel bad enough about this it's okay to keep doing it". This is a dangerous course of action because the damage to our self-respect from not living according to our core values is such that we will keep sending ourselves stronger and stronger messages to get our own attention. We may eventually create a crisis like disease, divorce, bankruptcy and so on.

Guilt

Peg: One time I thought I was in love with someone other than my husband and that I wanted to leave my marriage. I was sure that this was what I wanted and that my husband was a jerk. I had it all planned. I was going to tell him while we were on vacation that I was leaving him as soon as we got back. But I couldn't do it. I mean that literally. Every time I prepared to say it my throat would close, I would get dizzy and I would feel tremendously guilty. My heart knew I truly loved my husband, that I was just hurt and angry and not wanting to feel that.

***My head** thought I should leave and go with this guy who seemed to be so much more what a husband should be. And I* *wanted to blame the mess my relationship was in all on my husband. Not only that, I had witnesses to prove that I was right about him!*

My heart knew I truly loved my husband, that I was just hurt and angry and not wanting to feel that.

My soul wanted me to stay and be responsible in my marriage so that I could get off the cycle of failed relationships in my life.

My guilt was slowing me down long enough so that I would pay attention. At the time it wasn't clear to me. All I knew was that I felt crazy and would not leave my husband.

Most decisions come out of emotions. Even though we think we are making decisions from our rational, logical selves, we are not. The heart is always involved even if we are not aware of it. In fact people who are the most cerebral, are the most controlled by their emotions because their emotions go underground and unconsciously rule the roost.

Roger was the oldest child of a large family when his father died. He became the "man of the family" at twelve. His mother relied heavily on him.

Later as an adult, he worked for a large commercial airline company that was taken over by a man whose management practices were ruthless and alienated a large number of the company's employees.

Some of the disgruntled employees left and started their own company. Roger became its Chief Executive Officer. He was a very intelligent, capable man but the airline did not succeed — partly because of Roger's resentment of his old boss and partly because some of his decisions were made by the 12-year-old boy whose father had died. His unconscious need to do everything alone, to take care of his "family" took precedence over his conscious intention to do whatever was necessary to create a successful company. Roger was not aware of either of these influences on his decision-making processes.

Integrating the information from our heads, hearts and souls leads to clarity in our decisions and choices and power in our personal lives.

Make sure you allow time and space to hear all your messages and to learn from all of them.

Information outside us

There are three major sources of information outside us: support from others, mass consciousness and universal consciousness.

Support from others

Support from others is important when we have decided to make a change in our lives and our fear of and resistance to that change is threatening enough to stop us changing. The feelings we experience during change are so uncomfortable that we will do anything to make them stop: pretend that we have already done it or that we do not really want to do it or that someone else is making us do it. It is then that the support of other people, who are aware of what we decided to change, is essential. Their job is to remind us of our choice, and to tell us the truth about what they see us doing.

Peg: When I decided to be responsible in my relationship with my husband, I hated a lot of what I discovered about myself. For instance I wanted my way all the time and would throw a fit if I didn't get it and that's what I always accused him of! I didn't like to see things like that about myself because it was so uncomfortable. When I was making this change to be personally responsible, I needed my friends to tell me how they saw me acting in the relationship and to remind me that I chose to go through this for my own self-respect and freedom. This helped me to not blame and to stay on course. It was important that they be totally honest with me because if they had said something to make me feel better it would not have helped. It was important for me to ask only those people for support who would be equal with me and not try to take care of me.

Usually the greater the changes we desire, the greater our resistance. We may want to fight the support our friends give us.

Judith: A group of participants recently told me how they saw me handling a personal life situation. My defenses got so strong that I was very tempted to pull rank and act like a teacher. It was so difficult for me to hear what they were really saying. Instead I took a deep breath and dove in. I appreciate their courage.

We need to take what others say to us into our hearts and let their words affect our feelings. And it is not easy. It is a gift to ourselves. We need to take in what others say to us and experience it without either acting on it or discarding it. When our way of thinking is challenged we go into our survival mode and our position gets stronger and more intense.

Killing the messenger is not wise.

To take support that goes against our way of thinking feels like dying and it is. It is the death of an old pattern. When that really happens, there is a physical effect. The matter from the suppressed feelings from the old belief systems leave. It is a time when we may get sick.

To give support to someone else means always treating them equally. It means speaking our truth no matter how much we fear doing so. We allow ourselves to have our experience and everyone else to have theirs. It also means we do not offer support to anyone who has not asked for it. There is no reason to sacrifice ourselves.

Peg: Judith and I used to go around giving support to everyone, whether they asked for it or not. It was a big mistake! People got angry at us and always expected that we would tell them what to do. We finally learned to mind our own business, unless someone asked us.

Support is recognizing and treating everyone as equal and choosing their own life.

Mass consciousness

Mass consciousness is the conglomerate of beliefs and thoughts of our families, our culture and of humanity in general. It is like having radio signals aimed at our heads all the time and it affects us whether we are aware of it or not. Those radio signals vibrate in us like feelings except they vibrate in our heads, not our bodies.

Mass consciousness

There are patterns of behavior that are associated with different roles in this conglomerate and unless we consciously choose something else we will operate in these patterns because their pull is very strong and familiar. This mass consciousness has patterns for raising children, running a business, fighting a war, loving and everything else we do in our lives. For example there is a pattern associated with marriage. When we decide to get married that pattern clicks in and we start to treat ourselves and our lovers differently than we did before marriage. We stop seeing them clearly and start to see "husband" and "wife" instead. In the mass consciousness a "husband" is supposed to make money and provide for the "wife" and "children" and know about the world. A "wife" is supposed to cook, clean, take care of the "husband's" emotional and physical needs, raise the "children" and sometimes bring in additional income. People hurt themselves and their relationships trying to fit into this pattern even when what they really want to have in their marriages may be something totally different. Some wives make more money than their husbands. Some husbands would rather stay home with the kids and are better suited than their wives to do so.

Universal consciousness

Universal consciousness is another kettle of fish entirely. It is not created by the human mind, but originates in the combined soul of all that is. Some people refer to their originator as God. Others call that information their higher self or inner voice. This consciousness is the universal source of information about *what is so*, without judgement. There is no judgement involved. This source of information is not accepted as true by most of us. Into this realm taps telepathy, precognition and intuition, just knowing something is so without any logical explanation for it. The way to tap into this information is through personal responsibility and unconditional love. The context for universal consciousness is personal responsibility and unconditional love. Did you ever think about someone and have them ring you up just as you were thinking of them? Or know something was going to happen just before it did?

How does that happen? It is not always random or coincidental. You have switched radio stations momentarily. You have tuned into the universal consciousness station.

Universal consciousness

Universal consciousness always creates the biggest picture. It is where science and mysticism begin to merge. The inspiration that we call genius taps into universal consciousness. Copernicus, Aristotle and Einstein tapped that source for their genius and inspiration. It is how we know that loving ourselves and treating our bodies with respect will affect the environment of the planet. It is how inner peace creates global peace.

Anyone can tune into universal consciousness if heads and hearts are connected. We have a direct line and it is effortless. How do we know if a piece of information comes from universal consciousness? When our heads and hearts are integrated, the information we receive will feel true and make sense. Then it is a good idea to test it. After a while you will know from how your body feels.

Tapping into the universal source of information is easier than we might think and we all have had experiences with it. We may have discounted the information, however, because it did not match what our heads told us or because we felt too uncomfortable.

Peg: I love to see shooting stars. One night I was walking down my road in the country hoping to see some. I had heard there were to be meteor showers that night. I saw one fairly dim one and was on my way home when I "knew" that I should turn around and wait. I did and within a minute I saw a gorgeous shooting star.

EXERCISE: Remember the times that you have just known something was going to happen and it did, or some other instances of "knowing". Remember any times that you "knew" something and you ignored it. What was the result?

Knowing things can be as mundane as knowing when the traffic light will change, where to find a parking spot, or that there is a speed trap around the bend. It can be as useful as knowing who to trust in a business deal or when the weather is going to turn. And sometimes it can save your life.

113

A woman named Katherine had a grandmother who was scheduled to fly up to visit her on a particular flight. The grandmother called her and told her that she was changing to a later flight because she had a nagging feeling that the earlier flight was not a good idea. She was embarrassed but decided to trust her intuition. The original plane crashed and there were only a few survivors.

11

━ C H A P T E R ━
THE MODEL FOR CHANGE

Okay, you have read this book and you love the information. Some of it is upsetting. Some of it sounds a little far out. But it FEELS true and satisfies something deep inside. And as you have read the book, you see things in your life that you would like to change. Ah, change! The very word can make our minds tremble. We all have to deal with change these days: we change, our friends change, our lovers change, our business changes, the economy changes, the world changes. How can we deal with all this change without going crazy? How do we carry through with a change that we desire to effect without getting sidetracked and losing our way?

This chapter is about how to change, the structure and nature of change and some tools to help us in the process. It is a map, as it were, for change: what works and what does not. The map is generic and is true for how change occurs in an individual, a relationship, an organization or a society.

You did the guided meditation. You reconnected with your purpose. In order to fulfil your purpose, it needs to be translated into a form that can be manifested. It needs to be made into a vision. Your vision is a picture of your soul's purpose brought to life. Your vision belongs to you. Other people may have similar visions and similar purposes but yours is unique to you.

Your vision will inspire you in times of despair and mundane boredom. It will be a light to steer by when your travel is clouded with fog. It will be a motivating force to empower you to grow, no matter how you feel, and it will keep you focused on the biggest picture possible.

What is your vision and how do you want to accomplish it?

Now, it may take more than a moment to create your vision and mission. When you do, the model for change will guide you through the changes you will need to make to have it happen.

The model

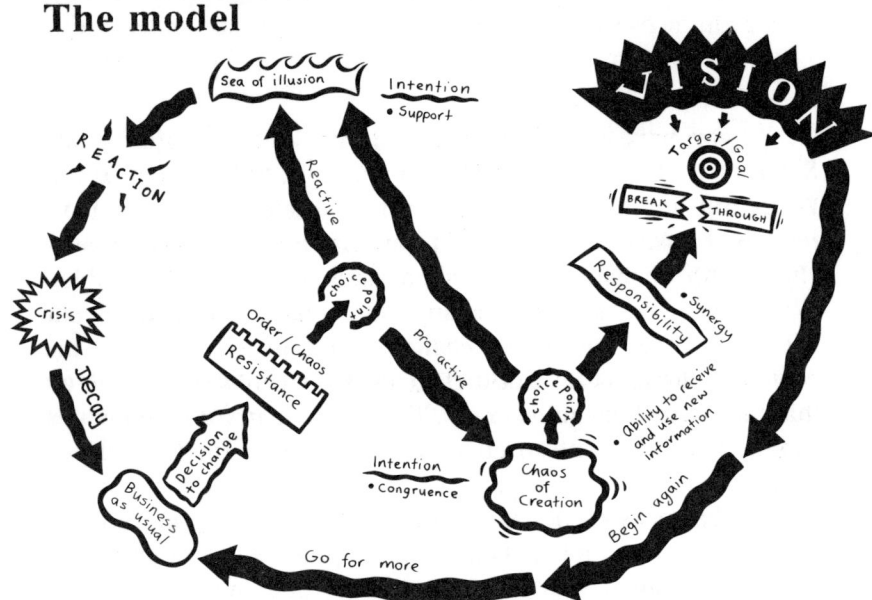

Step 1 We *decide* to change, to leave what is. The decision is made best with a clear vision and needs strong intention to carry it through. It does not matter if the change is prompted by an inner desire or an external situation. For example:

Personal	Relationship	Business
We decide to lose ten kilograms	We decide to get married	We decide to implement employee quality control

Step 2 Whammo! And our inner *resistance* to the change hits us really strongly. We want to go back to where we were, even though we want to change. For example:

Personal	Relationship	Business
We start to over-eat	Our lover's annoying little habits become all we see	We begin to think our employees are incapable of controlling quality

Step 3 Our decision to change and our resistance are equally balanced. If our decision were stronger we would just do it. If our resistance were stronger we would stop changing. This is a time when the *balance of order and chaos* (status quo and change) creates immense agitation. (Many people associate order with a positive situation and chaos with a negative one. In this model for change, the relative value has to do with the possibility for CHANGE. In the place of order there is no room for change. In chaos there is the option to change.) For example:

Personal	Relationship	Business
We hate ourselves for being fat but cannot seem to stop eating	We want to get married but are afraid it is a big mistake	We know that we want to implement the program but are afraid to give up our personal control

Step 4 If the agitation gets strong enough we move to a *choice point* — we either retreat to our history or move forward into the unknown. For example:

Personal	Relationship	Business
Keep the weight or lose it	Get married or not	Keep things the same or put in the new program

Step 5 Choosing to go for the past does not work. If the past were workable there would be no need to change in the first place. It results in an *illusion*, a deception of ourselves. Either we deceive ourselves into thinking that the change was not necessary or we say that we have already accomplished it. The self-deception has a grave effect in that it erodes our self-esteem. For example:

Personal	Relationship	Business
We buy larger size clothes; have our mother tell us we were too thin before	We decide that our lover is not marriage material but great for sex	We tell ourselves and our employees that they are responsible for quality but we do not act that way

Step 6 When we choose illusion often we cannot see what we are doing. We create a *crisis*. This is to wake us up to the changes we need to make. If we ignore the crises often enough, decay and death follow. On the other hand, we can be so shaken up by the

crisis that we recommit ourselves to our intention to change, and mean it. For example:

Personal	Relationship	Business
We have a heart attack. If the cycle continues it can result in death	Our lover leaves us. This can be repeated in relationship after relationship	Our employees become dispirited, lose respect for us, and production falls — could eventually mean business failure

Step 7 The other option is to risk the unknown and do something new, to stay with our intention to change. This choice throws us into the *chaos of creation*: chaos because we feel all the feelings that were protected by our old pattern; creation because it is literally that. We are in new territory and we are choosing our reality from the raw material of our experience in the moment. When we do this, we are in *paradox* — the state of maintaining two seemingly opposite experiences at once. We feel pulled in opposite directions: one, the life of comfort, the old familiar way of behaving; the other, the pull to our vision, a new way of being. We must be able to contain the past and create the future simultaneously by the focus of our will to stay. It is tricky but it is the key to success. For example:

Personal	Relationship	Business
We begin eating differently and exercising. All the feelings protected by the weight (anger, inadequacy, fear) are now felt	We plan the wedding. Even though we feel trapped, afraid, doubtful, not sure we want to be stuck with just one lover forever, afraid to be that vulnerable	We implement the worker quality control program. We feel how afraid we are that things will get really out of hand if we do not watch everything ourselves

Step 8 Chaos is extremely uncomfortable and the desire to bolt over to illusion becomes strong. Another *choice point* occurs. Will we go back or go on? It is now that *support* is critical — in the middle of chaos. It is easy to lose sight of our vision of where we are going or to fool ourselves about where we are. Support from our peers who know our intention and vision helps keep us in that uncomfortable, fertile chaos of creation.

Step 9 If we stay in the chaos of creation long enough and maintain our experience (paradox), we come to the next step on the model for change — *responsibility*. We become the source of our experience and we accept all information without judgement. This is a *big deal*: *we change the way we see*. The same data mean something different than they did before. This allows for new solutions to old problems. For example:

Personal	Relationship	Business
We understand the purpose the weight served: protection from getting hurt or from being seen as a sexual being	We see how much we want the relationship and how afraid we are to want that much	We see how the need to control covers a fear of not being good enough, and also great loneliness

Step 10 A curious thing happens at this point. We get so close to having what we want *we often stop* just short of actually reaching our goal because things are not as we pictured they would be. It may be that what we expected it to feel like or look like is not the way it is. Maybe we do not recognize it. Maybe we do not feel worthy to have what we want. Whatever our reason, many people, couples and businesses get 98 per cent of the way to their goal and stop. For example:

Personal	Relationship	Business
Our bodies are feeling good. People are starting to notice us. But we feel a loss and do not understand it	Our relationship is good. The wedding is upon us. But it is not satisfying somehow	Our employees are really taking to the new system. Profits are up. We feel unnecessary

Step 11 At this point we need to remember what our intention was. We need to stay congruent. We need to use everything we have learned! So it is okay if it does not look and feel as we expected! We need to call for support. We need to see the pull of illusion. If we really take that support, we will *break through* to a place of success. We will be in *integrity*, in a state of totally unimpaired ability — true to our deepest self and able to do whatever we set out to do. For example:

Personal	Relationship	Business.
We have compassion for our need for protection and realize that any change feels like loss for a while	We decide to be married, not just get married	We are free to be much more creative since we have responsible employees

This model for change works. The more it is used the easier it gets and the more powerful we become. But more importantly, it can support us to live with joy and self-respect.

EXERCISE: Remember what your soul told you was your purpose for living? Ask it again.

Your vision is the picture of your purpose brought to life.

If you were doing your purpose here what would it look like?

What would your body be like?

What would your relationship be like?

What would your business be like?

What business would you be in?

What changes would you be making in your life?

12
— CHAPTER —
THE BIG PICTURE

The need for personal responsibility and the demand for it to happen *right now* is very strong in the world at this time.

Change is occurring at a very rapid pace, whether it be in the relationships between countries, parents and children, or lovers and friends. These changes are happening so quickly, that we need to be personally responsible in order for peace to have a chance. We can no longer blame other people for what we are feeling and for what has happened in our lives.

Science is rediscovering that we are not separate from our environment and each other. Whatever we do as individuals affects everyone. How we treat our inner environment affects the earth's environment. In order to continue as a species our hearts and minds must be connected in every action we take. We can no longer make choices from logic or reasonableness alone. It is now time to make a quantum jump to achieve a new order of self to ensure our children a safe and loving world.

Personal responsibility and unconditional love are the cornerstones of this new reality. To be personally responsible for our actions and the results we create is to be liberated from our history. In his 1990 New Year's Day address to the people of Czechoslovakia, President Vaclav Havel, spoke about how each individual contributed to what happened there:

"...all of us are responsible, each to a different degree, for keeping the totalitarian machine running. None of us is merely a victim of it, because all of us helped to create it together."
From "The Great Moral Stake of the Moment", Newsweek, 15 January 1990, p.42.

That is true in a larger sense as well. All of us help create everything together.

The present rapid acceleration of change is symbolized by the concept of choice. As a species, we are at a choice point.

Individual choice has global impact.

It extends its results to the farthest reaches of the universe. We have the privilege as humans to choose our beliefs, our behavior and our world. We are at the crossroads of being able to access our deep inner knowing, our intuition, by the choices we make and the actions we take from moment to moment. We do not have to wait for a crisis before we act. We do not have to suffer a major loss such as a death, relationship failure, war or the total laying waste of the planet to propel us to grow. We really just need to choose.

We must also be aware that every time we move towards a greater consciousness and clarity, there is an equal and opposite opportunity for unconsciousness and confusion. As the possibilities for peace, abundance and health become increasingly available, so do the possibilities for war, famine and disease. Is it an accident that the reunification of Germany and Iraq's invasion of Kuwait occurred simultaneously? Or that the possibilities for democracy within the Soviet Union come hand-in-hand with economic collapse and dire food shortages?

We are in a paradox of global proportions. It is what one man can do and it is all of us or none, as John Denver says. We have the ability to restore this world to a Garden of Eden and live in harmony with ourselves, each other and the earth. We also have the capability to destroy ourselves, each other and possibly wound our mother earth beyond even her powers to heal.

Which way will we choose? Buckminster Fuller believed that humanity passed through a crisis at the time of the Falklands dispute: that we could have tested the effects of a limited nuclear war in a relatively isolated section of the planet, and we chose not to. We are at a similar place now. And since individual choice has global impact, the options of war, famine and disease or peace, abundance and health become our individual responsibility.

What will we each choose in our personal lives? We have a daily opportunity to choose which life we will live.

EXERCISE: Close your eyes and imagine yourself lying peacefully on your deathbed. As you lie there, you review the choices you have made in your life. You ask yourself:

- **What are my joys?**
- **What are my regrets?**
- **What would I choose to do differently?**
- **What would I choose to treat differently?**
- **How would I choose to live my life if I had to do it all over again?**

(The above exercise has been reproduced with kind permission of Diana Shulman, PhD.)

Choice means freedom.

This book is directed to those of you who are actively seeking freedom inside yourselves no matter what the source of your desire, whether it is a conscious awareness of what freedom really means or whether it stems from a chronic dissatisfaction that cannot be abated. The information in this book is one path to freedom. Use it.

Reread now the Guided Meditation in the Introduction. Go in peace.

SUGGESTED READING

Bateson, Gregory (1972). *Steps to an Ecology of Mind: A Revolutionary Approach to Man's Understanding of Himself.* Ballantine Books: New York.

Chilton Pearce, Joseph (1971). *The Crack in the Cosmic Egg: Challenging Constructs of Mind & Reality.* Pocket Books: New York.

Chilton Pearce, Joseph (1977). *Magical Child. Rediscovering Nature's Plan for Our Children.* Bantam: Toronto.

Ferguson, Marilyn (1980). *The Aquarian Conspiracy: Personal and Social Transformation in the 1980s.* J.P. Tarcher: Los Angeles.

Frankl, Victor (1978). *Man's Search for Meaning.* Hodder and Stoughton: London.

Freud, Sigmund 1917–1933. (1966). *Complete Introductory Lectures on Psychoanalysis,* translated and edited by James Strachey, W. W. Norten & Co: New York.

Fuller, Buckminster (1969). *Ideas and Integrities.* Collier Books: New York.

Gawain, Shakti (1986). *Living in the Light: A Guide to Personal and Planetary Transformation.* Whatever Publishing: Mill Valley, California.

Hay, Louise L. (1988). *Heal Your Body.* Hay House: Santa Monica, California.

Jung, C.G. (1933 first published). *Modern Man in Search of a Soul.* (Translated by W.S. Dell and Cary F. Baynes) Harvest/Harcourt Brace Jovanovich: San Diego.

Levenson, Dr Frederick B. (1985). *The Causes and Prevention of Cancer.* Stein and Day: New York.

Millman, Dan. (1980). *The Way of the Peaceful Warrior*. H.J. Kramer, Tiburon, California.

Perls, Frederick, Hefferline, Ralf F., Goodman, Paul (1951). *Gestalt Therapy. Excitement and Growth in the Human Personality*. Dell: New York.

Peters, Tom. (1988). *Thriving on Chaos*. Alfred A. Knopf: New York.

Prigogine, Ilya and Stengers, Isabelle (1984). *Order out of Chaos: Man's New Dialogue with Nature*. Bantam Books: Toronto/New York.

Roberts, Jane (1974). *The Nature of Personal Reality*. Bantam Books: Toronto.

Siegel, Bernie S. (1986). *Love, Medicine & Miracles*. Harper & Row: New York.

Verny, Thomas and Kelly, Tom. (1982). *The Secret Life of the Unborn Child*. Dell: New York.

Wolf, Fred Alan (1984). *Star Wave: Mind, Consciousness, and Quantum Physics — An original interpretation of what quantum physics tells us about the human mind*. Macmillan: New York.

Wolf, Fred Alan. (1986). *The Body Quantum — The New Physics of Body, Mind and Health*. Macmillan: New York.

Zukav, Gary. (1989). *The Seat of the Soul*. Simon and Schuster: New York.

Zukav, Gary. (1980). *The Dancing Wu Li Masters: An Overview of the New Physics*. Bantam Books: New York.

BIOGRAPHICAL NOTES

In the beginning
Judith
When I was four years old, I lost a mitten. I had a very difficult time losing anything. To me everything had consciousness and was alive. All I could think of was that the lost mitten would be so lonely without its pair and how lonely it must feel. Another poignant memory was feeling sorry for Cinderella's step-sisters. I thought they were maligned and had a raw deal.

All through my growing years, I concerned myself with being connected. I felt as if I was that lost mitten and one of Cinderella's step-sisters.

My family focused a great deal on my dad's health and his business. My parents were frightened and angry a lot of the time. Yet we never really shared our feelings with each other. They believed in "protecting the children" but I was able to see what was going on without their saying anything.

My teenage years were difficult. My parents were still being protective and afraid, and wanted to control my social life. I rebelled. There were many fights and fearful times.

In my mid-twenties, I found it hard to distinguish between what was true and what was illusion. I had two children and felt terrified of the responsibility of being a mother and wife. I was unable to feel happy as a married woman and chose to divorce when my children were two and four years old. I knew that the way I was in my life would be transferred to my children. So I began a search to discover what makes people do what they do, what makes them take the choices that they do. It was a personal quest: to trust myself to know what I felt and what was true.

During the Viet Nam war I began working for Horizon House, a psychiatric halfway house in Philadelphia, which was a pioneer in community development with people who had been hospitalised for many years. We had some tremendous success. I wrote a paper called "Some outcome data" published in *Advances in Behavior Therapy*, Academic Press, 1969. The main point was that no matter what the data or empirical information, the point of view of the researcher would affect the results of the study. My paper was published because it supported what people like Karl Popper were writing about.

At the University of Pennsylvania I ran a program called University Year for Action Program. It placed college students into different community projects and taught them how to adapt to the culture they were working in so that they could be successful. It taught them how to empower community people to take over the projects.

Then I went to Vermont where I helped found the college which is now called Burlington College, and founded the Psychology Department which at that time was a Transpersonal Psychology Program called New Genesis, teaching people how to integrate the mind, body, spirit and emotions. I was there for a number of years. Meanwhile I also taught in the University of Vermont in the College of Education. That is where in 1979 I got my Master's degree in the Foundations of Education, always searching, deeply, deeply searching for how people learn, why and what they learn, and still looking for answers to the essence of the question I had asked since I was four years old and had lost my mitten: what creates connection, what creates choice, what creates learning?

Peg

I grew up in a family where no one talked about feelings at all or dealt with what was happening in the family. Conversation was limited. In fact, I hardly remember even small talk. I felt afraid most of the time and I believed that my father was harsh and that my mother was wonderful. My whole childhood was based on somebody being good and somebody being bad. It was all black and white with lots of blame. There was never a question that I could be the source of what I was experiencing — it always came from the outside.

When I was twenty I got pregnant and then got married. We moved to Vermont and I lived in the same patterns of my childhood, where I would blame him just like I would blame my father for everything that was going on in me. I never accepted responsibility for any of it except perhaps that I was not willing to leave him.

Two to three years after we were married, something very powerful happened. I had come from Vermont to Miami to visit my mother, intending not to go back. I hated my marriage but I had not said anything to my husband. While there I had a miscarriage. I had not even known that I was pregnant. And all of a sudden I had to go back, even though I had planned not to. There was nothing outside me saying that I had to, there was nobody to pin that compulsion on. I was very confused by what was going on.

Our meeting

Peg

I went back to Vermont. Our marriage continued. At one point we had ten weeks of couple therapy with some clinical psychologists in Burlington, Vermont. It was what I call "trying to figure out who was doing what". It was very intellectual and nobody really talked about what was going on — just like my family. It was like band-aids. We felt soothed in our minds and left, but nothing really changed in our relationship.

A little while after that, the same clinical psychologists contacted us and said they wanted to start a center to train paraprofessionals to do psychotherapy and invited us to be the first trainees. In 1972 we started two days a week. It was like learning to swim by being thrown in at the deep end of the pool. There was a great deal of experience with proportionally little discussion of theory. I began to see things instinctively and knew what was happening in relationships.

In this largely experimental mode we learned an eclectic blend of many therapies, for example transactional analysis and Gestalt. When we discovered primal therapy I was excited by it because it fitted my pictures of what had happened to me — and I was very good at it. About this time, my husband and I divorced, and we both continued to work at the center.

We started another training program where about a dozen people did a program similar to the one my husband and I had done. Then Judith joined the Center for Change.

Judith

Even though I had just got my Master's Degree in Education, I still was not satisfied. I understood what happened to people, based on the psychological theories on what I learned in college, at the university and graduate school and what I saw in the programs I ran in the summers where group leaders were brought in from all over the country, including at that time the Esalon Institute, which was seen as the pioneer in the human potential movement in the USA.

I went to seminars and they still did not give me the information I desired. When I became a counsellor for the students at the college, I noticed that they kept repeating the same behaviors as if they needed to leave the forest they were living in, in order to be healed. But all they wanted to do was to jump from tree to tree in the same forest. They did not want to leave their homes. They did not want to leave their history.

I had heard about an opening at a place in Burlington called the Center for Change where they were doing some very avant-garde work, and where the top psychotherapists in the area were working. I decided to leave the college world and go into the world of therapy to see if there I could discover the basis from which people make choices.

That is where I met Peg, when I started working there in 1976. Among the group of partners Peg was the only one who seemed to hear what I would say to her, and she and I were really interested in sharing any new information we discovered.

I decided at that time to do EST (Erhart Seminar Trainings). That was where I had my first experience of knowing from deep within my heart, and understanding that all experience comes from the self — that the self creates its own interpretation of whatever is going on outside. From EST I started to understand that all events are neutral and that it is only in our interpretation of the external event that meaning comes into our lives.

Peg

When Judith joined the Center for Change in 1976 it was extremely disrupting because she talked about what was really going on. It was my first experience of anybody who talked about what was true instead of keeping to all the agreements that we make unconsciously or semiconsciously, to keep the status quo. It was a terrifying and wonderful experience.

The work we had been doing until then, while brilliant, only went up to a certain point. It really did not address what was going on at the deepest level so that people could make a permanent change. It acclimatised people to their choices and made those choices more palatable.

And here was this person who was outrageous, who would just say what was going on. She was not what you would call polite, but she was real. I was so drawn to that way of being, of just saying what was true, even though I was afraid of upsetting the way I had always operated. But the fear did not outweigh the desire to hear what she had to say because I recognized it as something unique in my experience.

From the world of therapy to the world of change

Judith

In 1979 my husband and I and another couple decided to open up a new place and we called it Carriage House Associates in Health.
We put together a holistic health organisation with therapy and

massage and acupuncture, again one of the new trends in the humanistic movement.

Peg, who had quit the therapy business for a few years, joined our staff in 1981. One of the main reasons for her coming was that we had decided to take all our information and our work out of the world of therapy and into the world of change, to teach people how to see what was truly occurring, what was really going on, to not analyze it but to see it, truly experience it, and then make a choice from the experience of how they wanted to live their lives.

The seeds of choices/synergy

Judith

We were experimenting and growing all the time, until there came a conflict in context. Peg and I and a number of other people from our Health Center attended a workshop called Money and You. Subsequently, all but one of our partners (we were seven in all) also attended the workshop. The experience of that workshop is what began the conflict. There was a division amongst the partners into two groups: those who believed, and wanted to live according to the idea, "that people are the source of their experience", and those who said that other people create how you feel. That fight grew and grew until eventually it destroyed the partnership and the company.

Peg

At the beginning of Money and You there were wonderful games and a lot of interesting information about the way the brain works, about what money really is and how you operate with money. It was great until the last game of the workshop, the Blocks Game. We divided into teams of five and the task was to demonstrate to a team of "receivers" the essence of certain words without talking. There were words like love, trust, synergy and mastery.

It took us from eight o'clock one evening until noon the following day to finish this game. It was a very passionate, wonderful, horrible, frustrating and powerful experience.

The second part of the game was to demonstrate the essence of responsibility. We had no idea what that meant at first. We thought it meant keeping your agreements and picking up after yourself, and being a good person. The receivers kept rejecting this idea and we were enraged and wanted to kill them.

Finally, after much agitation Judith and I reached a place that was totally unexpected. We no longer cared about winning the game. We were overwhelmed by our experience of being totally connected inside and out. There was no separation between us and anybody else in the room. In fact, it went past the room and included everyone. There was no place where we ended and somebody else started. That was the experience of responsibility: we were connected and we were the source of what was going on; it did not matter what the receivers did; it did not matter what our team members did; nothing mattered.

Only Judith and I had that experience. We wanted more than anything else for that experience to be common in our lives, for that feeling of fluid light and connectedness to continue. In order for that to happen we had to give up blame and see ourselves as responsible for our experience. We wanted our business partners to feel this way too. Unfortunately they didn't. They had not shared our experience in that workshop. They did not understand what we were talking about, and did not want to operate the way we wanted them to. And we had a hard time accepting that.

In search of more

Judith

It was as if we were fanatics. We really became what fanatics are. We just wanted everyone to understand what we experienced. We did not realise at that time, nor for a while afterwards, that people have to experience it themselves. You cannot really explain it.

But that time of unconditional love and the experience of responsibility was the source of the work we have done since.

Peg

We decided to recreate the experience we had in that original workshop of Money and You into a training about choice, about laughter and joy, about being real. That is what the information in this book is about.

You learn intellectually, spiritually, emotionally and physically that you are the source of everything that you perceive in your world. To the position of personal responsibility we add unconditional love, total acceptance of self, so that all parts of the human become integrated. We support people to become the essence of their vision. And that is what this book is about — how to truly become the essence of your vision.